BONNIE AND CLYDE

BONNIE AND CLYDE

A Biography

Nate Hendley

GREENWOOD BIOGRAPHIES

GREENWOOD PRESS
WESTPORT, CONNECTICUT • LONDON

Library of Congress Cataloging-in-Publication Data

Hendley, Nate.
    Bonnie and Clyde : a biography / Nate Hendley.
        p. cm.—(Greenwood biographies, ISSN 1540–4900)
    Includes bibliographical references (p.) and index.
    ISBN-13: 978–0–313–33871–7 (alk. paper)
    ISBN-10: 0–313–33871–X (alk. paper)
    1. Parker, Bonnie, 1910–1934. 2. Barrow, Clyde, 1909–1934.
3. Criminals—United States—Biography. I. Title.
    HV6245.H46   2007
    364.15'52092273—dc22
    [B]   2007003238

British Library Cataloguing in Publication Data is available.

Library of Congress Catalog Card Number: 2007003238
ISBN-13: 978–0–313–33871–7
ISBN-10: 0–313–33871–X
ISSN: 1540–4900

First published in 2007

Greenwood Press, 88 Post Road West, Westport, CT 06881
An imprint of Greenwood Publishing Group, Inc.
www.greenwood.com

Printed in the United States of America

The paper used in this book complies with the
Permanent Paper Standard issued by the National
Information Standards Organization (Z39.48–1984).

10 9 8 7 6 5 4 3 2 1

Every reasonable effort has been made to trace the owners of copyright materials in this
book, but in some instances this has proven impossible. The author and publisher will be
glad to receive information leading to more complete acknowledgments in subsequent
printings of the book, and in the meantime, extend their apologies for any omissions.

To the 12 known dead:
John Bucher
Eugene Moore
Howard Hall
Doyle Johnson
Malcolm Davis
Harry McGinnis
Wes Harryman
Henry Humphrey
Joseph Crowson
E. B. Wheeler
H. D. Murphy
Cal Campbell

CONTENTS

Photo essay begins after page 60.

SERIES FOREWORD

In response to high school and public library needs, Greenwood developed this distinguished series of full-length biographies specifically for student use. Prepared by field experts and professionals, these engaging biographies are tailored for high school students who need challenging yet accessible biographies. Ideal for secondary school assignments, the length, format, and subject areas are designed to meet educators' requirements and students' interests.

Greenwood offers an extensive selection of biographies spanning all curriculum related subject areas including social studies, the sciences, literature and the arts, history and politics, as well as popular culture, covering public figures and famous personalities from all time periods and backgrounds, both historic and contemporary, who have made an impact on American and/or world culture. Greenwood biographies were chosen based on comprehensive feedback from librarians and educators. Consideration was given to both curriculum relevance and inherent interest. The result is an intriguing mix of the well known and the unexpected, the saints and sinners from long-ago history and contemporary pop culture. Readers will find a wide array of subject choices from fascinating crime figures like Al Capone to inspiring pioneers like Margaret Mead, from the greatest minds of our time like Stephen Hawking to the most amazing success stories of our day like J. K. Rowling. While the emphasis is on fact, not glorification, the books are meant to be fun to read. Each volume provides in-depth information about the subject's life from birth through childhood, the teen years, and adulthood. A thorough account relates family background and education, traces personal and professional influences, and explores struggles, accomplishments, and contributions. A timeline highlights the most significant life events against a historical perspective. Bibliographies supplement the reference value of each volume.

PREFACE

This book is about Bonnie and Clyde, America's most notorious criminal couple. In addition to detailing their crimes, I examine the social, economic, and family backgrounds of both of these outlaws. I hope this information will allow for a greater understanding of the era and the criminals it produced. Technology—in the form of fast cars and automatic weapons—also plays a major role in this book. The dangers posed when criminals have better equipment than police are still highly relevant today.

Sources for more information on cars, guns, and American history have been cited throughout. In addition, I offer the URLs for several Web sites that contain fascinating and often overlooked material on Bonnie and Clyde.

The Internet offers a bounty of Bonnie and Clyde information, for those who know where to look for it. Many Barrow gang–related sites contain reproductions of original newspaper articles from the 1930s. These articles offer valuable insight into Bonnie and Clyde and their impact in the states they rampaged through. Such articles are also interesting to read from a journalistic and historical perspective. As a writer, I found that locating Bonnie and Clyde clippings online made my research enormously easier.

The Internet has also made readily available documents that normally would be almost impossible to track down. The confession made by W. D. Jones (one of Bonnie and Clyde's earliest criminal companions) to Dallas police comes to mind. It's doubtful that an author would ever publish the entire confession in a book on Bonnie and Clyde. With this in mind, I was very pleased to find the confession online. Since I used it, however, the document appears to have vanished into the ether. Fortunately, a link to a site containing W. D. Jones's famous 1968 interview with *Playboy* magazine is still in working order.

For anyone interested, the Internet also offers such memorabilia as a census form listing Clyde's family, school photos of Bonnie and Clyde, a document detailing a "conditional pardon" to Henry Methvin (another criminal associate), etc. For the morbidly inclined, grisly photographs taken after Bonnie and Clyde's violent deaths can also be located online.

One of the things that intrigued me the most about Bonnie and Clyde was how media-savvy they were. We tend to think of celebrity criminals as a modern phenomenon. Not true. Like many Depression-era bandits, Bonnie and Clyde were very aware of their public image. They loved to take pictures of each other armed to the teeth and menacing the camera. They loved the attention that the media bestowed on their crimes. It would have probably pleased them to know that a film about their lives was one of the biggest hits of the 1960s. That the movie was full of inaccuracies and distortions likely wouldn't have bothered them. It was the enduring myth that counted.

Bonnie, the poet laureate of the Barrow gang, would have also appreciated the vast number of books that have been written about her and Clyde. I am extremely grateful to the authors who have come before me. I found John Treherne's *The Strange History of Bonnie and Clyde* and Bryan Burrough's *Public Enemies* to be particularly helpful. Both of these books offered good insights with a minimum of moralizing. *I'm Frank Hamer*, the biography of the controversial Texas Ranger who pursued Bonnie and Clyde, is an excellent source of quotes from Hamer who rarely talked to reporters in his lifetime. Although the book has some weaknesses, *I'm Frank Hamer* remains essential reading. Crime historians and Bonnie and Clyde experts recommend reading *Ambush* by Ted Hinton (another member of the posse that tracked down the Barrow gang) as a counterpoint to *I'm Frank Hamer*.

For an understanding of the cultural, economic, historic, and political times of the 1930s, John Steinbeck's *The Grapes of Wrath* is indispensable. Although it's fiction, *Grapes* gives an incredibly vivid picture of the era. In many ways, Bonnie and Clyde were similar to the "Okies" of Steinbeck's novel. Except that Steinbeck's characters tried to escape poverty by driving to California while Clyde preferred to rob and kill.

If Bonnie and Clyde's case offers a lesson in sociology, it is also intriguing for its psychological aspects. Was Clyde a sociopath—violent, impulsive, unworried about consequences, and unable to feel empathy for his victims? What then was Bonnie? Was she also a sociopath, or was she simply so narcissistic and wrapped up in notions of love that she was able to overlook the fact her lover was a sadistic brute? Perhaps she was just bored with working-class life in Texas, and teamed up with Clyde for some thrills.

I have tried to present opposing viewpoints, where possible. Like many famous criminal cases, the pursuit of Bonnie and Clyde has become laden with legends and myth. Some of the main participants in the Barrow gang saga lied or offered misleading takes on what really happened. I have done my best to sort out facts from falsehood.

I have also tried to avoid glamorizing or demonizing Bonnie and Clyde. It's easy to make the pair heroic or demonic, depending on your perspective. Some sources, for example, have painted the two as a Depression-era Robin Hood and Maid Marian—a righteous outlaw stealing from rich folks to benefit the poor and his faithful female companion. At another extreme, Bonnie and Clyde have also been compared to Ian Brady and Myra Hindley, a hideous boyfriend-girlfriend team from 1960s Britain who tortured and killed little kids for fun.

In truth, Bonnie and Clyde were a rather ordinary pair of individuals who just happened to murder a whole lot of people. This, more than anything, is the most frightening aspect of their short lives and violent crimes.

Since they are best known as "Bonnie and Clyde," not "Parker and Barrow," I have referred to Bonnie Parker and Clyde Barrow by their first names throughout this book. I have also referred to members of Bonnie and Clyde's gang by their first names. Everyone else is referred to by the last name upon second and subsequent mention.

I would like to thank the Greenwood Publishing Group for asking me to write this book. I would also like to thank several individuals, including L. J. "Boots" Hinton, Debborah Moss, Rick Mattix, Jim Knight, and Frank Ballinger, who provided excellent information into the true Bonnie and Clyde story. I also want to thank my wife, Alyson, for her infinite patience, faith, and love.

BONNIE AND CLYDE: AN INTRODUCTION

Bonnie Parker and Clyde Barrow were outlaws who terrorized the U.S. Southwest and Midwest during the early 1930s. They are also the most famous criminal couple in American history. There are museums that catalogue their misdeeds and movies that depict their lives. On the Internet, a plethora of Web sites offer photographs, news stories, police bulletins, and other information about Bonnie and Clyde's brief crime spree.

Considering the extent of their renown, it's ironic that Bonnie and Clyde built their reputation on petty thievery. The pair primarily robbed small-town grocery stores and gas stations, rather than banks. The Barrow gang, as the group of misfits who coalesced around Clyde was called, never carried out any major heists. Their biggest "take" was under $10,000. In Bonnie and Clyde's case, crime did not pay very much.

For much of the time, Bonnie and Clyde and their gang members lived like bums, eating and sleeping in their car and bathing in country streams. Other criminals, such as John Dillinger, were scornful of the Barrow gang. Dillinger thought they gave a bad name to holdup artists.

If they never made any particularly profitable robberies, the Barrow crew was proficient at murder. They were responsible for at least a dozen homicides. Bonnie and Clyde's main victims were policemen, usually gunned down in panic and haste.

Ruthless and reckless, Bonnie and Clyde were also incredibly lucky. On numerous occasions they managed to evade overwhelming attacks by the police. They had a remarkable ability to escape from the most hopeless of situations. A cartoon from the *Dallas Journal*, published in

April 1934, depicts a befuddled lawman, watching numerous miniature cars marked "Barrow" driving in and out of a series of holes.[1] The Barrow gang's sheer audacity was also breathtaking. One of Clyde's most successful criminal ventures involved breaking *into* a prison (to rescue a comrade) rather than breaking out.

Like top celebrities, Bonnie and Clyde were very much aware of their image. They constantly took photographs of themselves, posing with high-powered weapons. The Bonnie and Clyde photo album depicts a handsome, if slight, dark-haired young man, and a pixie-like young woman (Bonnie weighed less than 100 pounds). One famous picture shows tiny Bonnie "sticking up" Clyde with a shotgun. The gun is practically as long as her arm. Another classic snapshot shows Bonnie striking a pose in front of a car. She stands with a pistol against her hip, foot on the car bumper and a cigar in her mouth—the very image of a Hollywood gangster's *moll*. Bonnie came to hate this photo, after it became widely circulated. The cigar, she indignantly explained, was a prop. Real ladies (and Bonnie classed herself as such) didn't smoke stogies.

Bonnie and Clyde shared similar roots. They both came from poor, white families in rural, southern communities. Poverty made Clyde hungry for money. He wanted to get rich by the fastest route possible, which in his case meant taking other people's cash at gunpoint.

Of equal importance to their legend is the fact Bonnie and Clyde hailed from Texas, America's most mythologized state. Texas had been the home of any number of larger-than-life characters, such as Judge Roy Bean, Belle Starr, Sam Houston, and Davy Crockett. Texas has long prided itself on certain values, including independence, toughness, and self-reliance.

Texan history is notable for extremes of violence and justice. The state was born out of a bitter struggle with Mexico. This struggle climaxed with the Battle of the Alamo, an 1836 encounter that pitted a tiny band of settlers against Mexican infantry. After the Civil War, Texas became part of "the Wild West"—an arid stretch of the U.S. Southwest infamous for bandits, gun battles, and showdowns at high noon. Bank robbers such as Sam Boss and John Wesley Hardin terrorized Texan communities during this period.

The Wild West legacy underpinned another notable feature of Texas, past and present: the application of swift, brutal punishment for law-breakers. The nineteenth century saw the emergence of the Texas Rangers, a super-tough band of police praised for cracking down on criminals. Like the Texas Rangers, Clyde Barrow was self-reliant, independent, and quick to resort to violence if need be. Like outlaws of the Wild West, Clyde was also a sadistic killer, who valued guns and mobility.

Clyde's weapon of choice was the Browning Automatic Rifle (BAR). Designed for military use, the BAR could shoot 20 rounds in less than three seconds. With a single pull of the trigger, Clyde could deliver more firepower than the entire Jesse James gang combined. When it came to transportation, Clyde favored Ford V-8s. These vehicles were rugged, reliable, and fast. Clyde was so impressed he allegedly sent a letter to the Ford Motor Company, praising their automobiles.[2] Clyde's choice of weapons and transportation gave the Barrow gang an enormous advantage over law-enforcement agencies.

Bonnie and Clyde were cutting-edge criminals operating in a rural environment that had barely advanced from the nineteenth century. Few American farms had electricity in the early 1930s and horses were still used to transport people and crops. Telephones weren't common in country residences. Police departments in rural and small-town communities were understaffed and underfunded, if not downright incompetent. Archaic laws made it difficult for police officers to chase criminals across state or county lines. Local cops couldn't rely on a powerful federal presence to help them out either. As late as 1933, agents from the Federal Bureau of Investigation (FBI) weren't allowed to carry guns or make arrests.[3]

Bonnie and Clyde thrived in this milieu. Using fast Ford V-8s, they could zip from community to community and make speedy getaways. Clyde's preference for BARs meant that the Barrow gang was usually better-equipped than most small-town police departments.

Bonnie and Clyde weren't the only criminals to take advantage of fast cars and powerful guns. The Depression featured an explosion in violent crime. Savage criminals such as John Dillinger, the notorious Barker family, Pretty Boy Floyd, Baby Face Nelson, and Machine Gun Kelly became household names.[4]

Thanks to the Depression, many out-of-work Americans came to see these outlaws as heroes, fighting back against the corrupt forces of money and power. While a large segment of the public clamored for law and order, another segment thrilled to the exploits of outlaws in their midst.

The presence of Bonnie Parker added a curious, contemporary twist to the Barrow gang's exploits. Unlike Clyde, Bonnie was not a young offender who fell into crime almost as a habit. By all accounts, she was an intelligent, high-spirited girl brought up by a normal, loving family. Bonnie always remained close to her family, risking arrest or capture to visit her kin. All sources agree that Bonnie was deeply in love with Clyde. It's unclear how smitten Clyde was in return.

If Bonnie was loving and loyal to Clyde, the exact nature of her role in the Barrow gang is open to dispute. Some movies and books have portrayed Bonnie as the real boss of the Barrow crew, ordering around a meek and mild Clyde. As intriguing as they are, such depictions aren't accurate. Captured members of the Barrow gang always insisted that Clyde led and Bonnie followed. Clyde Barrow was the undisputed leader of the gang that bore his name.

Some of Bonnie's criminal cohorts say she never even fired a gun, much less killed anyone. Other witnesses depict her as a gun-loving shrew, who laughed as she killed two badly wounded motorcycle policemen lying helplessly by a Texas highway.

The extent of Bonnie's private relationship with Clyde has also been grounds for much speculation. It's not even clear if they were lovers, as well as partners in crime. Some historical accounts offer lurid portraits of a nymphomaniac Bonnie, seducing the male members of the Barrow gang when Clyde couldn't please her. Other accounts depict Clyde as gay or impotent—more interested in guns than sex.

Regardless of her private relations with Clyde, it was clear that Bonnie was no ordinary moll. While she deferred to Clyde's leadership, she wasn't submissive or subservient. Unlike Blanche, the wife of Clyde's older brother, Buck, Bonnie wasn't prone to hysterics. She didn't lose her cool, even when caught in a police ambush. She was willing to risk death and jail to stay with Clyde. She was always by his side, even during shootouts.

It was this "stand-by-your-man" quality that separated Bonnie from other female felons of the Depression. "Most so-called 'gun molls' were never more than mistresses or wives, and rarely took part in the action," notes crime writer and historian Rick Mattix.[5] Without Bonnie, Clyde would have been regarded as a two-bit cop-killer with a grudge against society.

Indeed, on its own, Clyde's story isn't all that remarkable: Poor kid grows up rough in Texas. Commits crimes. Gets caught. Commits bigger crimes. Commits multiple homicides. Is eventually gunned down by police. The presence of such a steadfast, spunky woman by his side humanized Clyde (who was otherwise a fairly cold, unpleasant person) and dramatized his run from the law. The public was attracted by the notion of a pair of lovers who were also outlaws, even as they condemned their crimes. "I think the notion of a boy-girl bandit team struck some kind of romantic chord with a lot of people," notes Mattix.[6]

Aside from the Barker family (whose matriarch, Ma Barker, may or may not have been the brains of the operation), Clyde is the only famous outlaw of the 1930s whose name is always associated with that of his ladylove. Good thing too, because when he wasn't shooting people or carrying out crimes, Clyde was a relatively bland person. His motivation was straightforward: He was too lazy to work and preferred to steal. Most of the people Clyde killed were peace officers or store clerks. Clyde didn't kill them because of any deep-rooted psychological trauma; they were just simply in the way. He shot cops because he didn't want to go to jail. Bonnie added color to Clyde's otherwise gray-toned personality.

Two of the Barrow gang's biggest shootouts happened at hotels, where Bonnie and Clyde plus family members and associates, had taken up temporary residence. Living as an extended family, as it were. In both of these cases Bonnie showed her mettle by either shooting it out with police or actively helping Clyde escape.

Bonnie was arguably the smartest member of the Barrow gang. She certainly was the most artistically inclined. Two poems she wrote helped cement Bonnie and Clyde's legend. These works make good use of rhyming verse and criminal lingo to glorify the Barrow crew. One poem, entitled, "The Story of Bonnie and Clyde," became widely published following the death of its subjects. The poem rather falsely glorifies its subjects, portraying them as poor, put-upon folks striking back against oppressive police. Clyde comes across as downright noble in this work, an admirable person, not a low-life criminal. No matter. Bonnie's verses firmly became entrenched in the popular consciousness, even if they were nothing more than fantasy.

Frank Hamer, who makes up the final piece in the Barrow gang saga, offers another reason why Bonnie and Clyde remain so well known today. Frank Hamer was a figure steeped in mythology. He was the most famous member of a famous police organization (the Texas Rangers). Hamer killed virtually dozens of criminals in his career and handed down justice in a firm, two-fisted style. His real-life exploits seem like something from a Hollywood Western. He was brought into the Bonnie and Clyde case in the same manner that a Mafia family might hire a freelance hit man for a particularly tough assassination. By hiring Hamer, the state of Texas was basically admitting they had given up trying to capture Bonnie and Clyde alive. Even more remarkable, Hamer had carte blanche from the highest levels of the Texas government to pursue the case as he saw fit.

Hamer succeeded where other lawmen had failed. He brought the Barrow gang's crime spree to a close, with a brutal ambush on a Louisiana country road. This ambush marked the end of Bonnie and Clyde's criminal career and their entry into legend.

NOTES

1. Editorial cartoon, *Dallas Journal*, April 9, 1934.

2. For a look at the letter Clyde Barrow allegedly wrote to the Ford Motor Company, see http://texashideout.tripod.com/bc.htm or John Treherne, *The Strange History of Bonnie and Clyde* (Briarcliff Manor, N.Y.: Cooper Square Press, 1984), p. 95.

3. For more information on the FBI, see www.fbi.gov.

4. For a comprehensive history of Depression-era outlaws, see Brian Burrough, *Public Enemies: America's Greatest Crime Wave and the Birth of the FBI, 1933–1934* (New York: Penguin Books, 2004). For a more concise history, see Stone Wallace, *Dustbowl Desperadoes: Gangsters of the Dirty '30s* (Edmonton, Alb.: Folk Lore Publishing, 2003).

5. Rick Mattix, e-mail interviews with author, November 14–22, 2006.

6. Ibid.

TIMELINE: EVENTS IN THE LIFE OF BONNIE AND CLYDE

1909	Clyde Barrow is born in Telico, Texas, on March 24.
1910	Bonnie Parker is born in Rowena, Texas, on October 1.
1914	Parker family moves to Dallas.
1921	Barrow family moves to Dallas.
1926	Bonnie marries Roy Thornton. Clyde and his brother, Buck, are arrested for stealing turkeys. Clyde is released. Buck spends a few days in jail.
1928	Bonnie begins working as a waitress in Dallas area restaurants and cafes.
1929	Clyde and Buck are arrested for committing robberies and released on bail. Roy Thornton is arrested for robbery. Buck is rearrested and given a five-year jail sentence.
January 1930	Bonnie and Clyde meet for the first time (exact date is in dispute).
February 1930	Clyde is arrested for robbery.
March 1930	Bonnie smuggles a pistol into the Waco prison and Clyde uses it to escape. That same month, Buck Barrow escapes from Huntsville prison. On March 19, Clyde is captured in Ohio.
April 1930	Clyde is imprisoned at Eastham prison farm (one of Huntsville state penitentiary's 11 farms). He allegedly commits his first murder while in Eastham.

July 1931	Buck Barrow marries Blanche Caldwell.
December 1931	Barrow voluntarily turns himself in to the law. He is convinced to do so by his wife, who did not know her husband was a fugitive until weeks into the marriage.
January 1932	Desperate to get out of work detail, Clyde has a fellow convict lop off two of his toes with an axe.
February 1932	After his mother pleads his case, Clyde is released on parole.
March 1932	The Barrow gang comes together for first time to rob a hardware store in Kaufman, Texas. Bonnie is caught and spends several weeks in jail.
April 1932	Clyde commits his first officially recorded murder. He kills storeowner John Bucher during a robbery in Hillsboro, Texas.
June 1932	Bonnie is released from jail. She teams up with Clyde and Raymond Hamilton to establish a hideout in Wichita Falls, Texas.
August 1932	The Barrow gang kills Sheriff Eugene Moore at an outdoor dance in Stringtown, Oklahoma.
October 1932	Clyde kills storekeeper Howard Hall in Sherman, Texas.
December 1932	Raymond Hamilton is arrested by police in Michigan. W. D. Jones, an old West Dallas acquaintance of Clyde's, replaces him in the Barrow gang. Along with W. D., Clyde murders Doyle Johnson, a young salesman enjoying the holidays with his family, in Temple, Texas, on Christmas Day, and steals his car.
January 1933	The Barrow gang kills Police Officer Malcolm Davis in Dallas. Bonnie and Clyde kidnap Police Constable Thomas Persell in Springfield, Missouri, but release him unharmed.
March 1933	Buck Barrow is released from prison. While Buck promises his wife, Blanche, he will go straight, he insists on meeting Clyde.
April 1933	The Joplin, Missouri, reunion between Clyde and Buck is interrupted by the arrival of police. Two peace officers, Wesley Harryman and Harry McGinnis, are killed.

June 1933	Bonnie is seriously burned and injured during a car accident in rural Texas. A week later, the Barrow gang murders Marshal Henry Humphrey in Alma, Arkansas.
July 1933	The gang is involved in another shootout with police in Platte City, Missouri, on July 19. Buck is seriously wounded, and Blanche is partly blinded by flying glass. Five days after the Platte City ambush, a huge posse intercepts the Barrow gang near Dexter, Iowa. Buck and Blanche are captured, and he dies a few days later.
August 1933	Raymond Hamilton is transferred to Eastham prison farm, to serve out a 263-year sentence.
September 1933	In Platte City, Blanche pleads guilty to the charges against her and is sentenced to receive 10 years at a women's prison in Missouri.
November 1933	Police ambush Bonnie and Clyde in Dallas but fail to kill or capture the elusive outlaws.
January 1934	The Barrow gang breaks into Eastham on January 16 to free Raymond Hamilton. Prison guard Joseph Crowson is killed during the breakout. Four other prisoners, including Henry Methvin, escape with Raymond.
March 1934	Following serious personality clashes, Raymond splits off from Clyde.
April 1934	On Easter Sunday, Clyde and Henry Methvin kill two highway policemen, E. B. Wheeler and H. D. Murphy, near Grapevine, Texas. According to legend, Bonnie administers the coup de grâce to the fallen officers, shooting them in the head at point-blank range. A few days later, Clyde and Henry kill another policeman, Constable Calvin Campbell, in Oklahoma. They kidnap Campbell's boss, Police Chief Percy Boyd, and drive him around, but release him unharmed. The same month, Raymond Hamilton is arrested in Sherman, Texas.
May 1934	Bonnie and Clyde have their last reunion with family members in the Dallas area. On May 23, 1934, a posse consisting of Frank Hamer, Sheriff Henderson Jordan, and Deputy Prentiss

Oakley kills Bonnie and Clyde in a bloody ambush near Gibsland, Louisiana.

1967   Release of the hugely successful and highly controversial movie *Bonnie and Clyde*, starring Faye Dunaway and Warren Beatty as the two famous outlaws.

1968   W. D. Jones gives extensive interview to *Playboy* magazine about his time in the Barrow gang. His interview is shaped into an article.

Chapter 1

OUTLAWS AND LOVERS

Clyde Barrow was hungry.

A skinny boy, not quite a teenager, Barrow walked around his family's yard, thinking about food. The yard was actually a patch of dirt and weeds underneath one of the arches of the Houston Street Viaduct in West Dallas. There, Henry Barrow, an illiterate tenant farmer and his worn-down wife, Cumie Barrow, had set up a makeshift camp. Other families, too poor to rent a house in Dallas proper, had also established rough homesteads beneath the viaduct. These homesteads consisted of makeshift wooden shacks and tents, giving the area the look of a gypsy encampment. The general neighborhood around the viaduct and beyond had a name. It was called "the Bog" on account of the nearby Trinity River, a muddy expanse of water that occasionally flooded the area.

Short, thin and jug-eared, Clyde had dark hair and handsome, almost feminine, features. He didn't seem to mind living in the Bog. After all, he had experienced far worse in his short life.

Clyde Barrow was born on March 24, 1909, in Telico, Texas. His parents had eight children in total (Clyde was number six). They lived on a farm a few miles outside Telico proper. A tiny speck on the vast, flat landscape, Telico had a population of maybe 100 people. It was situated about 30 miles from Dallas. The Barrow farm was broken down and decrepit and provided a bare subsistence living for the family. The black-earth prairie around Telico was notable for scorching hot summers and stifling winds. The Barrow clan grew cotton and corn and raised cows, pigs, and chickens.

The rural society in which Clyde was raised was primitive by contemporary standards: Running water, modern plumbing, and motorcars were all relative luxuries. Farmers still made do with well water, privies, and horses. Most farms didn't even have electricity; as late as the mid-1930s, only 1 American farm in 10 was electrified. In Texas, that figure stood as low as 2 percent. The big utility companies didn't think it was profitable to establish power lines in the relatively poor backcountry. U.S. farms wouldn't get electricity until the New Deal.[1]

Farmers got by with candles and kerosene and other basic energy sources, such as firewood. This sounds cheery but it wasn't, considering all the modern implements powered by electricity, including refrigerators, stoves, and furnaces. As for air conditioners, they didn't exist yet. Farmers in Texas and elsewhere had to bear the full brunt of the brutal summer sun, without recourse to artificial cooling systems.

It was a society only a few years removed from the Wild West. Clyde grew up hearing tales about "folk hero" outlaws such as Jesse James (in reality, an embittered pro-Confederate murderer) and Cole Younger. One of his very few childhood pleasures was seeing movies at a local theatre. Many of these films were Westerns, depicting gunfights and horseback chases through the Southwestern landscape.

Such was the environment Clyde Barrow grew up in. No wonder he was excited, at age 12, when the Barrow family moved to West Dallas. Living under a viaduct seemed preferable to scratching out an existence on a bleak farm in the Texas prairie. Henry Barrow was convinced the move would improve his family's station. He scoured the area for work while his kids explored the Bog.

An adventurous boy, Clyde already had a reputation for mischief, if not outright delinquency. One of his hobbies was torturing small animals. Back in Telico, this had taken the form of squeezing the neck of the family chickens until they were nearly dead. Clyde also enjoyed capturing birds and breaking their wings. He would laugh heartily as the crippled birds flopped around in the dust, pathetically trying to take flight.

There were fewer animals to torture in West Dallas, but more to explore. Clyde enjoyed walking around the encampment, investigating other family's hovels and meeting other kids his age. A few months after the Barrows turned up at the viaduct, the Jones family moved in. The Joneses had a six-year-old son named William Daniel. W. D., as he was later known, hero-worshipped Clyde. W. D. thought Clyde was captivating and charismatic. Clyde had no time for the boy, however, and generally ignored him. Clyde was more interested in hanging out with his own siblings. He was particularly close to his sister, Nell, and brother, Marvin Ivan. Nell and Marvin (who usually went by the nickname "Buck") were both older than Clyde.

The Barrows were lax when it came to disciplining their kids. Cumie and Henry never hit Clyde and rarely scolded him. This was because they were exhausted, not progressive-minded. The Barrow parents spent virtually all their time engaged in labor, whether it was preparing food, doing farm work (in Telico), or looking after the youngest kids. In Dallas, Henry took a job in an ironworks that occupied him most of the day.

Thanks to his new job, Henry was eventually able to move his family out of the viaduct and into a proper house in West Dallas. For a dirt-poor family, it was a monumental step up the social ladder. Henry later quit the ironworks and launched a combination gas station/grocery store. He continued to work extremely hard to provide for his family.

Clyde didn't share his father's work ethic. He was an indifferent student and hated school. He dropped out as soon as he legally could, at 16. Out of school, Clyde took a variety of low-paying jobs. At one point, he was employed as a messenger boy for Western Union (a telegram company). Telegrams consisted of very short messages, often just a few words. These messages would be transmitted from one telegram machine to another, via a network. Once a message had been received, it would be printed out on paper and delivered to the proper recipient by a messenger boy.

Clyde worked at Western Union and other jobs. He saved up his money and bought a car for $50. He also moved out of the Barrow household and in with his sister, Nell. By this point, Nell was married to a man named Cowan and had her own house. Cowan was a musician who was on the road a lot. Clyde amused himself by trying to learn how to play his brother-in-law's saxophone. Clyde was as apathetic at work as he had been at school. He liked having money but didn't want to strain himself earning it. He dated a high school girl named Anne and fantasized about marrying her. Thinking about Anne was a lot more fun than worrying about work.

The era in which Clyde came to manhood has been immortalized as the "Roaring Twenties"—a time of flappers (liberated young women with short hair); dance crazes; movie stars such as Charlie Chaplin, Mary Pickford, and Douglas Fairbanks, Jr.; jazz music; and general abandon. People wanted to forget about the misery and hardship of the First World War and have a good time.

Bootleg booze was the accelerant that fuelled the party. As of early 1920, it had become a crime to manufacture, sell, transport, export, import, or possess alcoholic beverages in the United States. Alcohol prohibition was widely ignored, however, as bootleggers smuggled in liquor from Canada or made it themselves in vile home stills. If Prohibition was a joke in the big cities, it was taken very seriously in rural areas and the South.

Small-town America was still very conservative. The Roaring Twenties didn't make much of a dent in this part of the country. The 1920s saw the resurgence of the Ku Klux Klan throughout the South and Midwest. The Klan despised blacks, Jews, Catholics, labor leaders, bootleggers, and immigrants from southern Europe. The KKK burned crosses and lynched people to enforce its extremely narrow, bigoted view of the world.

Clyde had no interest in politics; he was more concerned with personal matters. His relationship with Anne, for example, was starting to run into trouble. In the spring of 1926, Clyde had an argument with Anne, who subsequently stormed off to live with an aunt. Said aunt resided on a farm near San Augustine, Texas. This put her about 170 miles away from Dallas and her boyfriend. Angry and lovesick, Clyde was determined to see Anne and talk some sense into her. His own car wasn't in running order, so he rented a vehicle to visit his ladylove. With Anne's mother in tow, Clyde headed off to San Augustine. Anne and Clyde were soon reconciled. They made up, and spent several lazy days together, enjoying each other's company and plotting a future together.

Under the terms of his rental agreement, Clyde was supposed to return the vehicle within 24 hours. Once he teamed up with Anne, however, Clyde decided to ignore this contractual obligation. Back in Dallas, the car rental agency started getting nervous. The agency asked police to investigate why Clyde was taking so long returning its vehicle. The police tracked Clyde down on the farm where Anne's aunt lived. The cops confronted him and Clyde panicked. He probably could have talked his way out of trouble. Most lawmen would be sympathetic to the plight of a girl-crazed young man who wanted to visit his sweetheart. The cops might have let Clyde off with a warning. Instead of trying to sweet talk the constables, Clyde made a run for the woods. Not for the last time, the police chased Clyde but quickly lost him in the forested area around the farm.

Clyde stuck around the trees until the cops left. Then, he sheepishly made his way back to the farmhouse. Needless to say, Anne—to speak nothing of her mom and aunt—were not impressed. Clyde drove to Dallas under a black cloud. Ironically, once he got to Dallas, Clyde returned the vehicle without further incident. The rental agency was so pleased to get its car back that it didn't press charges. Clyde managed to avoid getting a criminal record, for the time being. In future years, Nell Cowan stoutly defended her brother. According to Nell, the car rental escapade was just a big misunderstanding. Nell believed the police had overreacted to what amounted to a harmless lark by a spirited young man.

Having learned nothing from his close call with the car rental agency, Clyde joined a band of delinquents back in Dallas. These miscreants called themselves "the Root Square Gang." They were fond of stealing car tires, which they would then sell in order to buy bootleg booze. The gang also tried its hand at burglary, and conducted a few small-time robberies. Once again, Clyde attracted the attention of local police. In December 1926, Clyde and his brother, Buck, were arrested for stealing turkeys. Clyde was let go, while Buck had to serve a few days in jail.

By this point, Anne's parents had become highly alarmed at their daughter's choice of suitors. They forced Anne to break off her relationship with the budding thief. If he was crushed, Clyde soon got over it. He began courting a new girl called Gladys, who lived in Wichita Falls, an oil town 120 miles outside of Dallas. To demonstrate his feelings for her, Clyde had her name tattooed on his arm. This tattoo complemented an already existing mark on his other arm, bearing Anne's name.[2]

Tattoos aside, Clyde wasn't a particularly impressive physical specimen. As a fully grown man, he only stood around five foot six and weighed less than 140 pounds. His frame was slight, his features soft. Photographs of him from this time depict a handsome, baby-faced young man with dark hair parted down the middle, as per the style of the day.

Clyde and Gladys decided to get secretly married, or so Clyde claimed. The alleged newlyweds moved into a house together in Dallas. Nell, whose own marriage had run into serious trouble, moved in with her brother. Clyde earned his keep by committing minor crimes, such as stealing cars. Nell soon moved out of Clyde's homestead, followed by Gladys. Clyde's sweetie moved back home with her family in Wichita Falls. Turns out Clyde and Gladys hadn't been married after all.

Clyde took the loss in stride. He was soon over Gladys and spent his time plotting the robbery of a local pharmacy. The pharmacy was duly robbed with the help of an unidentified accomplice. Clyde was delighted. Clyde and the accomplice teamed up with Buck and a second unidentified accomplice for bigger scores. The quartet didn't make any big heists, although they did manage to get arrested on suspicion of robbery. Police also suspected Clyde of several car thefts. Clyde, Buck, and the two accomplices posted bail and were temporarily released from jail.

In October 1929, the New York Stock Exchange experienced a cataclysmic meltdown, triggering a worldwide depression. That same month, the Barrow brothers and their unidentified sidekicks journeyed to a small town outside Dallas named Henrietta. There, they stole a car. The foursome drove this vehicle to another town, called Denton. In Denton, the quartet robbed a garage. Among other items, the crew removed a heavy safe from the premises and put it in their stolen car. With Clyde driving, the gang took off.

While motoring around Denton, Clyde became nervous. His erratic driving alerted police that something was up. Soon, a police cruiser was trailing the four men in the stolen car. Clyde began to panic. He hit the accelerator and tried to outrun the police. A chase ensued. Being a novice getaway driver, Clyde crashed the car into a tree, bringing the chase to an abrupt halt. In all the confusion, Clyde managed to get away from the crash site. Buck wasn't so lucky. Police arrested him on the spot and tossed him into jail, along with one of the accomplices. At his trial, Buck kept mum about his baby brother's involvement in the car and safe caper. Buck manfully accepted all the blame, a magnanimous thing to do considering Clyde's lousy driving had put him in this spot. Buck was sentenced to five years in the state penitentiary located in Huntsville, Texas. The accomplice got 10 years.

With Buck in jail, Clyde tried to sort out of his life. He had no interest in doing legitimate work. Crime was the only avenue that appealed to him. Unfortunately, he wasn't a very good criminal. Buck's incarceration was proof of that. None of this mattered to Clyde. He fantasized about pulling new crimes while Buck served out his sentence in Huntsville.

Like Clyde, Bonnie Parker was also born in rural Texas. She came into the world on October 1, 1910, in Rowena, a rural town of about 600 people, most of them farmers. Bonnie's mother was named Emma. Like Clyde's dad, Bonnie's father was named Henry.

Surface similarities aside, Bonnie had a much different upbringing from Clyde. Henry Parker worked as a bricklayer, which paid decently well. The Parkers were poor, but not desperate. Compared to the Barrow clan, Bonnie's family was practically wealthy. A hard worker, Henry Parker was devoted to his wife and kids. In addition to Bonnie, he had a son named Hubert (who went by the nickname "Buster") and a second daughter named Billie. Bonnie was the middle child, between Hubert and Billie.

Henry and Emma Parker were devoutly religious, which in rural Texas, meant they belonged to the Baptist church. The Parkers were tolerant and loving toward Bonnie, a healthy, high-spirited little girl. With light hair, fair skin, and big blue eyes and peppy manner, Bonnie was cute and charming.

In 1914, Henry died, and Bonnie's idyllic childhood came to an abrupt end. With three small kids to look after, Emma Parker was forced to move back in with her mother. Ma Parker lived in Cement City, a charmingly named community of rough homes built around a cement plant near Dallas. The neighborhood was rough and crime was rampant, but Emma had little choice. She took a job and left her kids with mom.

Bonnie soon recovered her spirits following the death of her dad and the unexpected move. She liked to pal up with her cousin, Bess, and raise hell. Bonnie and Bess, who was the daughter of Emma Parker's sister, tore around the neighborhood, causing mischief and starting small fires. The two girls nearly burned down Grandma Parker's garden fence. Only quick action on the part of the adults in the house saved the fence from going up in smoke.

Wild-child Bonnie remained ferociously devoted to her mother. When not raising hell, Bonnie tried to assist her mother out as much as she could manage. Bonnie was enrolled in school at age six. She proved to be a quick learner and won classroom prizes for her writing ability. Bonnie was petite, small-boned, and supremely confident. A show-off, Bonnie liked attention. In one notorious incident, Bonnie's antics broke up a school assembly. Bonnie was taking part in a show that required her to dress like a "pickaninny" (a white person's idea of what an African American child was supposed to look and act like, in those unenlightened times). She got annoyed, however, when a boy pulled her hat off. Clad in dark makeup to make her skin look black, Bonnie began to yell at the boy right on stage. The play—which was being watched by an audience of adults—fell apart in riotous assembly as Bonnie began doing gymnastic flips on stage.

Pretty Bonnie was popular with boys. They tried to win her favor with gifts of candy and gum. For years, Bonnie showed little interest in her masculine admirers. It wasn't clear whether she truly had no feelings for her wannabe boyfriends or was just displaying theatrical disdain. At age 15, Bonnie suddenly decided she was head over heels in love with a schoolmate named Roy Thornton. To demonstrate her love, Bonnie got a tattoo bearing Roy's name inked on her thigh. She married the young man at age 16. The newlyweds moved into a house situated a couple blocks away from Emma.

Bonnie had retained her childhood charms and pleasing appearance. She stood barely five feet tall and weighed less than 100 pounds. With her blonde hair and bubbly manner, she had a pixie-like appeal.

Bonnie's happiness at getting married was mixed with hysteria about leaving home. She suffered from intense separation anxiety and was loath to leave her mom. Bonnie kept in obsessive contact with her mom and often encouraged her to sleep over. Around 1927 or so, Roy started having second thoughts about his marriage. Bonnie's overwhelming need to be around her mother started grating on Roy's nerves. He began spending as much time as possible away from home. He would disappear for days on end without informing his wife where he was.

Bonnie started keeping a diary, which recorded her increasing unhappiness with Roy. Unfortunately for future historians, Bonnie only bothered to keep the diary for a few days. Her entry for New Year's Day 1928 was both schmaltzy and bathetic. She wrote, "The bells are ringing, the old year has gone and my heart has gone with it. I have been the happiest and most miserable woman this last year. I wish the old year would have taken my past with it. I mean all my memories, but I can't forget Roy. I am very blue tonight. No word from him. I feel he has gone for good…"[3]

As she pined for her husband, Bonnie took work as a waitress. She got a job at a downtown Dallas eatery called Marco's Café. Marco's was located on Main Street, close to the Dallas courthouse. Bonnie's customers included lawyers, cops, and municipal officials.

In early 1929, Roy returned from a nearly yearlong ramble. Bonnie had been faithful to her husband but was no longer madly in love with him. Their reunion was not a great success. With Emma Parker's approval, Bonnie ordered her husband out of the house for good. She had good reason for kicking him out, besides a broken heart. Roy had become a criminal. During his time away from home, he had worked as a burglar. By some accounts, Roy was a handy man with a blowtorch, an implement used to crack open bank vaults. Shortly after his ill-fated return to Dallas, Roy was arrested for robbery. The robbery in question had occurred in a small-town named Red Oak. Roy was found guilty and sentenced to five years in prison.

Marco's Café closed in November 1929. Bonnie quickly got another waitress job at a new café. She used her charms to ingratiate herself with the customers, particularly men. One of the café's patrons was a man named Ted Hinton. He would come to know Bonnie in a very different light over the next few years.

For unknown reasons, Bonnie quit her new waitress job. She was unable, however, to find new work. In early 1930, Bonnie went to live with a girlfriend in West Dallas. Her friend happened to have a broken arm so, like a good pal, Bonnie pitched in with the housework.

Accounts differ as to how Bonnie met Clyde. Some crime historians state that Clyde was a patron at a new restaurant Bonnie worked at in 1930. Other writers suggest they were first introduced at the home of Bonnie's broken-armed friend. Regardless of how they met, the two felt an instant connection. Bonnie viewed Clyde as handsome and charming. Clyde liked Bonnie's bouncy personality and elfin good looks. He felt like a giant standing next to her, which was good for his ego. The fact Bonnie was married to a jailbird and Clyde was a thief didn't impede the relationship. Bonnie and Clyde soon became an item. Being a family-oriented girl, Bonnie took Clyde to meet her mother. Emma Parker apparently was quite taken by Clyde. She later would describe him as likeable and good-looking. Clyde was soon staying as a guest in Emma's household.

Bonnie and Clyde's budding romance came to a sudden end when Clyde was arrested. Police suspected him of the robbery in Denton and a few other crimes in different cities. Bonnie was devastated and wrote to Clyde constantly while he was in remand. Once more, Clyde's luck held. Denton authorities decided they didn't have enough evidence against him to proceed with a trial. This victory was short-lived. The law still had its hooks into Clyde. He was transferred to Waco, Texas, and put on trial for car theft and burglary. Clyde was found guilty and given two years in jail, to be served at the state pen in Huntsville.

Bonnie had moved to Waco to be with Clyde during his trial. She stayed with a cousin named Mary who lived in that city. Bonnie frequently visited her man in jail. She also continued to write obsessively. One of her letters urged Clyde to reform his ways. It stated, "I want you to be a man, honey, and not a thug. I know you are good and I know you can make good." She also wrote, "This outside world is a swell place and we are young and should be happy like other boys and girls instead of being like we are."[4] It's unclear what Clyde thought of these missives. In addition to showing Bonnie's romantic side, her letters dispel the myth that she seduced him into a life of crime. This notion would later be put forth in B-movies and pulp novels based on Bonnie and Clyde's exploits.

Clyde discovered that one of his cellmates owned a pistol, but was loath to use it. The firearm in question was stored at the convict's house in East Waco. The prisoner mused out loud about the ethics of having his family smuggle the gun to him in jail. He was afraid his family members might get caught and punished. Clyde was less bothered by such scruples. He listened carefully as the convict explained the layout and location of his house. During visitor's day, Clyde passed this information on to Bonnie. He somehow convinced her to go to his cellmate's house, steal the firearm, and bring it to him in jail. Clyde hoped to use the weapon to break out. For all her letters imploring Clyde to give up the criminal life, Bonnie went right along with her boyfriend's plan. She probably saw it as a daring, romantic adventure. She would prove how much she loved Clyde by securing a gun for him.

In mid-March 1930, Bonnie and her very nervous cousin, Mary, went to the house of Clyde's cellmate. Clyde had told her when the convict's family would be out of the home. He'd also let her know where the convict had hidden a key. Key in hand, Bonnie and Mary let themselves into the home. The pair started searching for the pistol, which turned out to be more difficult to locate than anticipated. The gun was nowhere to be found. Bonnie and Mary turned the house upside down until the place looked like it had been burglarized. Finally, Bonnie and Mary managed to dig up the pistol, which turned out to be a small .32 caliber automatic.

Bonnie went back to Mary's place and set about figuring out a way to smuggle the weapon into the Waco jail. Bonnie had a flash of inspiration: She secured two belts around her lithe frame then carefully placed the pistol between them. She put her clothes on overtop the belts, then paid Clyde a visit.

The break-in had badly rattled cousin Mary's nerves. A few days after helping Bonnie steal a gun, Mary's anxiety rose anew when she read about a prison break in the newspapers. Reports stated that Clyde and two fellow convicts had broken out of Waco jail with the help of a smuggled pistol. Bonnie, for her part, was delighted to learn that her man was free. She talked about divorcing Roy Thornton, so she could become closer to Clyde.

Once he made it outside the prison, Clyde didn't try to hook up with his devoted sweetie. Instead, Clyde and his companions used the .32 to rob several gas stations and stores. Their crime spree soon came to a quick end after they were arrested in Middleton, Ohio. They were charged with robbing a dry cleaning store and the offices of a railroad firm. The three men had been outside prison for less than a month.

Clyde and his buddies refused to give the police any information. The cops soon established their identities, however, thanks to fingerprints. Clyde was hustled back to jail in Waco. His experiences encouraged Clyde to take up the pen and write a letter to Bonnie. His missive to Bonnie read, "I just read your sweet letter and I was sure glad to get it for I am awfully lonesome and blue."[5]

It appeared Clyde would remain lonesome and blue for some time. He was transferred from Waco to the state pen in Huntsville. Buck was not there to greet his younger brother, having recently broken out himself. Clyde was given a stiff sentence for escaping from jail: 14 years, to be served at Huntsville. Clyde glumly resigned himself to a long stretch behind bars. Bonnie continued to write him while Cumie Barrow pled with authorities to take mercy on her misguided son.

NOTES

1. Information on rural electrification can be found at Texas State Historical Association (TSHA) Online (www.tsha.utexas.edu), a self-described "digital gateway to Texas history at the University of Texas at Austin," and in the chapter, "TVA: Electricity for All," at the educational Web site, http://newdeal.feri.org/tva/tva10.htm.

2. The extremely informative Web site, http://texashideout.tripod.com/bc.htm, contains some of the only photographs in existence of Clyde showing off his tattoos.

3. For Bonnie Parker's diary entry, see John Treherne, *The Strange History of Bonnie and Clyde* (Briarcliff Manor, N.Y.: Cooper Square Press, 1984), p. 29.

4. Ibid., p. 54.

5. Ibid., p. 58.

Chapter 2

POETRY AND THE
PENITENTIARY

Huntsville state prison changed Clyde, as it changed everyone who entered the place.

Located 55 miles south of Dallas, Huntsville consisted of one main prison complex and 11 prison farms. The facility housed a total of 5,000 convicts at any one time. The main prison building boasted a Spanish-style façade and extremely grim living conditions. It was bug-ridden and deficient in all manner of supplies and equipment. Prisoners often only got a single blanket—and no mattress—to sleep on.

If conditions were bad in the main prison complex, then they were downright medieval on the farms. Some of the farms had no drainage and were strewn with garbage and accumulated human waste. Convicts were required to do heavy fieldwork. Any attempt to escape would be met by a bullet from the guards. Despite this, hundreds of prisoners tried to escape each year. Buck Barrow was one of them. He broke out of Huntsville in March 1930 and was still at large when Clyde showed up.

Prior to Clyde's arrival, Huntsville gained a new prison governor. His name was Lee Simmons and he was a decent, if extremely tough, man. He had the prisoners plant gardens to provide fresh fruit and vegetables to augment their squalid diets. Simmons ordered new facilities built to hold convicts and instructed the guards to tone down their discipline. Under Simmons, guards were no longer allowed to whip prisoners at will. Governor Simmons wasn't a sadist, but he wasn't a softie either. Guards still had the right to shoot escapees and use a two-foot leather strap to discipline unruly convicts.

Clyde arrived at Huntsville in chains on April 21, 1930. Upon admittance, Clyde was placed in the Eastham prison farm. This farm was considered particularly horrid even by Huntsville's low standards. The 13,000-acre spread was very isolated. Many of the prison's toughest, most dangerous inmates were put at Eastham.

At Eastham, Clyde had to join his fellow prisoners in doing manual labor in the hot sun. The convicts worked under armed supervision. One guard with a shotgun, sidearm, and bat stood watch. In the distance, another sentry, nicknamed the "long arm man," walked around with a high-powered rifle, ready to shoot in case of serious trouble. The addition of the "long arm man" was one of Governor Simmons's initiatives.

Among other chores, Clyde's work crew had to harvest cotton. The group moved among the fields, picking cotton like a gang of slaves from a previous century. This assignment proved especially onerous for Clyde. He hated manual labor and had no self-discipline. The boy who was never spanked by his parents found it extremely difficult to adjust to a regime of hard physical work. Making things more unpleasant was the tendency of the prisoners to fight among themselves. There are reports that Clyde's peers sexually abused him at Eastham. Certainly, the good-looking but slight young prisoner would have been a tempting target for stronger, more vicious inmates. One of Clyde's alleged assailants was a hardened con named Ed Crowder. At six feet and 200 pounds, "Big Ed," as he was called, towered over the more diminutive Clyde. According to L. J. "Boots" Hinton, son of famed lawman Ted Hinton, Crowder either attempted to sodomize Clyde or outright ravished him.

"Clyde didn't go for this, and reached for a lead pipe," states "Boots" Hinton.[1]

The pipe connected with Crowder's head, and the leering con fell down dead. A trustee allegedly took the pipe away and counseled Clyde never to speak of the incident. Crowder's body was decorated with stab wounds (administered by either Clyde or the trustee) to make it appear the man had died in a knife fight. Crowder's death was reported in newspapers, but wasn't blamed on Clyde. Guards didn't exactly strain themselves to solve the case.

"No one liked Big Ed," states "Boots" Hinton. "The inmates hated him," and the guards didn't like him either. Everyone "kind of thought [Crowder] got his just desserts." If true, then this incident marked "Clyde's first killing," says Hinton.[2]

Something else: If Clyde had been charged with killing Crowder, then the entire Barrow gang crime spree might never have taken place. A murder conviction might have led to the electric chair. At the least, Clyde would have remained behind bars at Huntsville, perhaps for the rest of his life. Crowder's murder has never been officially pinned on Clyde, however. Most Bonnie and Clyde biographers indicate his first homicide had yet to take place.

Attacks from fellow prisoners weren't the only thing Clyde had to deal with. The guards remained brutish and harsh, despite Governor Simmons's softening of the rules. They might not have been allowed to beat prisoners for no reason, but they could still inflict brutal corporal punishment for the slightest infraction. It was at Eastham, Nell Cowan would later claim, that her brother began to harbor a simmering hatred of authority, as personified by prison guards and cops. At night as he lay in his filthy bunk, Clyde dreamed of busting out of Eastham. It was a fantasy common to all prisoners, but with a twist. In Clyde's dreams, he broke out of jail, gathered up some guns then broke back *in*, to rescue as many prisoners as possible.

Loyal Nell visited Clyde often while he served his time. Bonnie was less consistent in her contact. While she regularly wrote to Clyde, she seemed to be blowing hot and cold on their relationship. She wasn't sure if she wanted to be romantically involved with a second man serving hard time.

Barrow family life continued apace, even with Clyde behind bars. In early July 1931, Buck Barrow married a pleasant backcountry girl named Blanche Caldwell. The ceremony was held in secret, given that Buck was still in hiding. Short, dark-haired, and attractive, Blanche was born in January 1911 and raised in Oklahoma. Photographs of Blanche show a perky young woman with a radiant smile. An only child, Blanche had been brought up in a religious environment. She had absorbed her spiritual lessons well. When Buck confessed, a few weeks into his marriage, that he was an escaped convict, Blanche didn't bolt. Instead, she was filled with missionary resolve. She would put her new husband on the path to the straight and narrow. To this end, Blanche pleaded with Buck to give himself up. In Blanche's view, Buck needed to finish his sentence in order to atone for his criminal past. Turning himself in would also prove he was serious about leading a moral life. Once Buck served the remainder of his time, he and Blanche could live in godly happiness and raise a family.[3] Blanche must have been convincing, for Buck agreed to surrender. On December 27, 1931, Buck journeyed to Huntsville and turned himself in. Prison officials were rather surprised but happily led him to a cell.

If Buck had gotten religion, his younger brother remained incorrigible. Prison life made Clyde so despondent he resorted to a desperate scheme to get out of work detail. He had a fellow convict lop off two of his toes with an axe (some crime historians say Clyde did the deed himself, but this isn't true). Newly crippled Clyde ended up in the prison hospital.

There, he quickly discovered his act of self-mutilation had been totally unnecessary. The whole time Clyde had been at Eastham, his mother had been lobbying for his release. She begged the legal authorities to free her son. Like Blanche, Cumie Barrow evidently possessed great powers of persuasion. In early 1932, while recovering from his foot injury, Clyde was informed he had been paroled.

Once he healed sufficiently, Clyde left the Huntsville prison. Hobbling around on crutches, Clyde bought some fancy clothes, cleaned himself up, then made a grand entrance at the Parker household. Bonnie was home, with a new boyfriend no less, when Clyde came calling. The boyfriend quickly made himself scarce and Bonnie and Clyde had a joyous reunion.

As happy as Clyde was to be back with Bonnie, the timing of his parole couldn't have been worse. The Stock Market crash of 1929 had led to a massive economic slump. By 1932, the country was in full grip of the Great Depression. Jobs were scarce for hardworking, law-abiding citizens, much less crippled ex-cons with dubious work habits. It was estimated that 10 million Americans were unemployed, while a further 30 million had virtually no income at all. Welfare as we know it today barely existed. Families on "relief" (i.e., receiving government assistance) were given paltry sums to subsist. It was feared that being too generous would encourage people to stay on relief instead of finding work. As a result, relief families often got under $3 a day. Admittedly, prices were cheaper during the 1930s, but three bucks was still barely enough to get by.[4]

Huge armies of vagrants (by some counts, as high as 2 million people) moved around the country, looking for work. These vagrants often jumped the rails and rode trains for free. They set up hobo camps, derisively called "Hoovervilles" after President Herbert Hoover, who seemed indifferent to the suffering and unable to stop it. Downtown sidewalks in major urban centers were packed with poor people selling stacks of fruit for pennies. Apple peddlers became a familiar sight, as the Depression grew worse.

People who still had jobs weren't much better off than their unemployed brethren. Thanks to the economic decline, wages had fallen dramatically. Manufacturers used the Depression as an excuse to cut salaries and benefits. Some sweatshops in New York City offered as little as 50 cents a week (terrible pay, even for the time). Workers who complained got fired. There were always jobless people willing to take their place.

Farmers were also hit hard. Agricultural prices dropped to the point where it became too expensive to harvest crops. It cost the farmers more to pick, sort, and transport fruits and vegetables than they could hope to gain back from their sale. The result was a rural apocalypse.

"In Montana, thousands of acres of wheat went uncut because they would not pay for the price of harvesting—16 bushels would earn enough to buy a four-dollar pair of shoes. In Iowa, a bushel of corn was worth less than a packet of chewing gum. Apples and peaches rotted in the orchards of Oregon and California, just as cotton did in the fields of Texas and Oklahoma. Western ranchers killed their cattle and sheep because they could not pay to feed them...In Kansas, farmers burned wheat to keep warm—a bushel now fetched only around $0.30 as compared to $3 in 1920," reads an account from the era.[5]

The situation in the Southwest was especially brutal. Poor farmers across the Southwest were violently evicted from their homes when they fell behind on their payments. Millions of disposed "Okies," "Arkies," and hillbillies (i.e., people from Oklahoma, Arkansas, Texas, and the South in general) gathered up all their possessions on old trucks and headed west. The highways were filled with caravans of poor people traveling to California in search of work.

John Steinbeck, in his classic novel, *The Grapes of Wrath*, immortalized the plight of the poverty-stricken Southwest. That novel features the travails of the Joad family as they make the long journey to the West Coast. Another book, called *Let Us Now Praise Famous Men*, captured images of real-life transients. Journalist James Agee and photographer Walker Evans compiled the book, which contained photos and stories of poor farmers in the South taken in the 1930s. The pictures were monumentally bleak—gritty black-and-white portraits of a people beaten down by poverty, hunger, and the sun.

The odds were stacked against Clyde finding legitimate work. Nonetheless, the Parker clan gave him the benefit of their doubt. Emma Parker informed Clyde he had her blessings to rekindle his relationship with Bonnie, provided he got a real job. Clyde indicated he wanted to go straight. He lounged around the Parker home for a few days until he was able to walk without crutches. Then, he traveled to Worcester, Massachusetts, for a construction job that Nell had arranged for him.

For a while, it looked like Clyde was serious about turning over a new leaf. He quickly became disenchanted with doing construction, however. After two weeks on the job, Clyde quit. He was tired and bored. Construction reminded Clyde of the oppressive fieldwork at Eastham. The legit world offered none of the thrills and excitement of crime. In the middle of March 1932, Clyde skulked back to Dallas. He immediately began chatting up Bonnie about another line of work he had in mind.

Shortly after Clyde's return, Bonnie made a bouncy announcement. Bonnie told her mom she had landed a new job demonstrating makeup and cosmetics in Houston. Emma was a bit surprised (this was the same daughter, after all, who couldn't stand to live apart from her mom, even in the same city). Mrs. Parker's surprise would have been amplified tenfold if she knew what Bonnie was really up to. Clyde had cooked up a scheme to conduct a robbery with a prison buddy named Ralph Fults. He wanted Bonnie to be involved in the caper. Bonnie eagerly went along, as she always did when Clyde suggested doing something.

The robbery was carried out—where exactly, it was unclear. Equally murky is what the trio was stealing. According to some accounts, the gang hit up a hardware store. In any case, things did not go according to plan. While making their escape from the crime scene, the vehicle Clyde was driving got stuck in mud. Clyde, Bonnie, and Ralph had to get out and make a run for it on foot. The thieves stumbled across muddy fields and dirt roads and eventually came across an unoccupied building, either a church or a barn (depending on who was recalling the story). Clyde left Bonnie at the building with explicit instructions to wait, while he and Ralph cast about for a new car to steal. Clyde promised he would come back and pick Bonnie up.

Bonnie did as she was told, for a while. She waited in the unoccupied building, but her man never returned. Clyde was apparently unable to find a suitable vehicle to steal. At one point, a police patrol came so close Bonnie could hear the cops calling out to each other. The police didn't search the building, however, and Bonnie remained undiscovered.

Bonnie waited and waited. After a few hours of this, she grew bored and decided to leave. She strode along a road and tried to hitchhike her way back to Dallas. She was spotted by police and picked up. Ralph was also caught at some point after the robbery, although Clyde, continuing his lucky streak, was not.

In late March 1932, Bonnie found herself locked up in Kaufman, a small rural community located just outside Dallas. The time in jail was not entirely unproductive. Bonnie, the winner of grade-school essay contests, took the time behind bars to practice her writing skills. She ground out a poem called "The Story of Suicide Sal." It was a colorful, narrative piece filled with underworld slang:

The Story of Suicide Sal

We each of us have a good "alibi"
For being down here in the "joint";

But few of them really are justified
If you get right down to the point.

You've heard of a woman's glory
Being spent on a "downright cur."
Still you can't always judge the story
As true, being told by her.

As long as I've stayed on this "island,"
And heard "confidence tales" from each "gal,"
Only one seemed interesting and truthful—
The story of "Suicide Sal."

Now "Sal" was a gal of rare beauty,
Though her features were coarse and tough;
She never once faltered from duty
To play on the "up and up."

"Sal" told me this tale on the evening
Before she was turned out "free,"
And I'll do my best to relate it
Just as she told it to me:

I was born on a ranch in Wyoming;
Not treated like Helen of Troy;
I was taught that "rods were rulers"
And "ranked" as a greasy cowboy.

Then I left my old home for the city
To play in its mad dizzy whirl
Not knowing how little of pity
It holds for a country girl.

There I fell for "the line" of a "henchman,"
A "professional killer" from "Chi";
I couldn't help loving him madly;
For him even now I would die.

One year we were desperately happy;
Our "ill gotten gains" we spent free;
I was taught the ways of the "underworld";
Jack was just like a "god" to me.

I got on the "F.B.A." payroll
To get the "inside lay" of the "job";
The bank was "turning big money"!
It looked like a "cinch" for the "mob."

Eighty grand without even a "rumble"—
Jack was last with the "loot" at the door,
When the "teller" dead-aimed a revolver
From where they forced him to lie on the floor.

I knew I had only a moment
He would surely get Jack as he ran;
So I "staged" a "big fade out" beside him
And knocked the forty-five out of his hand.

They "rapped me down big" at the station,
And informed me that I'd get the blame
For the "dramatic stunt" pulled on the "teller"
Looked to them too much like a "game."

The "police" called it a "frame-up,"
Said it was an "inside job,"
But I steadily denied any knowledge
Or dealings with "underworld mobs."

The "gang" hired a couple of lawyers
The best "fixers" in any man's town,
But it takes more than lawyers and money
When Uncle Sam starts "shaking you down."

I was charged as a "scion of gangland"
And tried for my wages of sin;
The "dirty dozen" found me guilty—
From five to fifty years in the pen.

I took the "rap" like good people,
And never one "squawk" did I make.
Jack "dropped himself" on the promise
That we make a "sensational break."

Well, to shorten a sad lengthy story,
Five years have gone over my head
Without even so much as a letter—
At first I thought he was dead.

But not long ago I discovered
From a gal in the joint named Lyle
That Jack and his "moll" had "got over"
And were living in true "gangster style."

If he had returned to me sometime,
Though he hadn't a cent to give,
I'd forget all this hell that he's caused me,
And love him as long as I live.

But there's no chance of his ever coming,
For he and his moll have no fears
But that I will die in this prison,
Or "flatten" this fifty years.

Tomorrow I'll be on the "outside"
And I'll "drop myself" on it today:
I'll bump "em" if they have me the "hotsquat"
On this island out here in the bay...

The iron doors swung wide open next morning
For a gruesome woman of waste,
Who at last had a chance to "fix it."
Murder showed in her cynical face.

Not long ago I read in the paper
That a gal on the East Side got "hot"
And when the smoke finally retreated
Two of gangdom were found "on the spot."

It related the colorful story
Of a "jilted gangster gal."
Two days later, a "sub-gun" ended
The story of "Suicide Sal."[6]

by Bonnie Parker

The poem makes it clear that Suicide Sal is a victim and her criminal friend, Jack, is a heel. The verses didn't seem to reflect Bonnie's true feelings at the time, however. She had no intention of dumping Clyde, even though he was responsible for her being in jail.

With Bonnie in jail, Clyde continued his criminal spree. In the spring of 1932, he robbed the Sims Oil Company in Dallas. He also teamed up with a fellow crook named Raymond Hamilton. A short, light-haired young man, Raymond was chatty and extroverted. Together, Clyde and Raymond plotted new capers.

John Bucher groaned as the two men called out for him from the street outside his house. It was close to midnight on April 27 and Bucher needed his sleep. A 61-year-old churchgoer and entrepreneur, Bucher was also a good businessman. The customer came first, even if he arrived in the middle of the night. Bucher ran a combination gas station, jewelry store, and grocery in the small town of Hillsboro, Texas, located 45 miles southwest of Dallas. Bucher and his wife, Madora (some books give her name as Martha), lived in an apartment above their combined enterprises.

Bucher recognized the men's voices. The two had been inside his business earlier that day. They had returned, so they said, to buy some guitar strings.[7] Why they needed to make this purchase in the middle of the night wasn't clear. The men stood in the street and called for Bucher to open up his shop. Grumbling, Bucher stuck his head out of a window and yelled that he would be down momentarily. He quickly threw on some clothes so he didn't have to greet his late-night customers in pajamas.

Bucher wasn't totally naïve; he grabbed a revolver before trundling downstairs and placed it in his belt. One had to be prepared for anything in his line of work. Bucher stepped into the darkened store on the first floor of his property. He turned on the lights, then unlocked the door, to let his unexpected customers inside. They were two white men, young and wide-awake. Bucher led them to the back of the store where he sold guitar strings behind a glass case.

One of the two strangers selected some appropriate strings and Bucher handed them over. The man offered a $10 bill in return. Bucher didn't have enough change for such a large bill. He would have to open the store safe to give the man the money he was owed. Tracing his forefinger on the grip of his gun, Bucher called up the stairs to Madora. He ordered her to come down and unlock the safe. It's likely that Bucher brought his wife down as a precautionary measure. That way, he could keep an eye on the two guitar-loving strangers while the safe was opened.

Madora did as she was told and came down the stairs and into the store. She glanced at the two young men standing before her husband. She also noticed the revolver in Bucher's belt. It didn't alarm her. Guns were common in rural Texas. Madora unlocked the safe so her husband could make change.

In return for opening the safe, one of the strangers pulled out a revolver and aimed it at John Bucher. Before Bucher could draw his own weapon, the stranger squeezed the trigger and fired. The sound of gunfire was deafening inside the crowded store. With her ears ringing, Madora watched in horror as her husband collapsed. He had been shot in the chest, and a bullet had entered his heart. He was probably dead before he even came into contact with the floor.

Reacting out of shock and instinct, Madora tried to grab her fallen husband's pistol. The two killers spotted this move and ordered Madora to place the weapon on the counter. This she did, as one of the two intruders stepped over Bucher's body to grab money and jewels from the safe. The cash on hand amounted to $15. The thieves were luckier in their choice of gems. The safe contained diamond rings, which the stranger eagerly scooped up. The man pocketed rings worth around $2,500. Madora knelt down to comfort her husband, not realizing he was dead already. The two killers raced out of the store.

The Hillsboro robbery marked Clyde's first official murder. It was also a sign of things to come: a low-stakes robbery and a totally innocent victim shot dead. Bucher was buried in Hillsboro while the police unsuccessfully tried to track down his killers.

Showing his true colors, Clyde ran back home to his parents following the shooting at Bucher's store. He hid out in the Barrow household and spun imaginative lies about what had transpired in Hillsboro. While Clyde admitted to Nell that he had taken part in the robbery, he denied being the triggerman. He insisted that Raymond Hamilton was the real killer, that all he had done was drive the getaway car. In light of Clyde's future, trigger-happy antics, this seems extremely doubtful. It's almost certain that Clyde was the man who gunned down John Bucher in cold blood. In the long list of victims of Bonnie and Clyde, John Bucher's name always comes up first (not counting Big Ed Crowder).

Subsequent accounts of the Hillsboro killing placed Bonnie on the scene. She was described as being either a getaway driver or a decoy, sent into the store to distract Bucher so Clyde and Raymond could hold up the place. These stories are false. While Clyde was committing murder, Bonnie was still languishing at the Kaufman jail. Emma Parker, meanwhile, was doing her best to get Bonnie released.

In mid-June 1932, Bonnie appeared before a grand jury. It was the jury's task to determine whether enough evidence existed to go forward with a trial against Bonnie. The evidence against Bonnie was weak. Bonnie also did a good job on the stand. Relying on her theatrical personality, Bonnie buttered up the jury with various sob stories. She convinced them she was really a good girl who inexplicably had been swept along in a robbery case. She offered excuses for her behavior and painted a portrait of a naïve waif unfairly persecuted by police for a crime she had no part in.

The jury bought it, and Bonnie was released from jail. Bonnie moved back in with her mother in Dallas. Mrs. Parker was most eager for Bonnie to break up with Clyde. Bonnie's experience at the Kaufman jail convinced Emma that Clyde was no good for her. Surprisingly, Bonnie agreed to ditch her new paramour. She said she wanted Clyde out of her life.

In late June, Bonnie took off for Wichita Falls (home of Clyde's old girlfriend, Gladys). She breezily explained to her mother that she was looking to land a new waitressing job. An oil town, Wichita did indeed have plenty of bars and restaurants, so this seemed like a reasonable enough explanation. What Bonnie didn't mention was that Clyde and Raymond Hamilton were also living in Wichita Falls. Clyde didn't seem to have a problem sharing a hideout with the man he accused of gunning down John Bucher.

Clyde and Raymond were renting a cottage in Wichita Falls and plotting new capers. Their latest brainstorm involved a robbery at the Neuhoff Packing Company in Dallas. Unlike the bloody robbery in Hillsboro, Clyde and Raymond took the time to plan this raid carefully. They even figured out an escape route and secured another hideout (an empty farmhouse in Grand Prairie, Texas).

In late July 1932, Clyde and Raymond drove Bonnie back to her mother's house in Dallas. Clyde tipped off Bonnie about his plans. He told her to listen to the radio on a particular day. If all went well, news of the robbery (and the thieves' getaway) would be reported over the airwaves.

On the given day, Bonnie kept her ears glued to the radio. She listened with delight as the announcer offered news of a holdup at the Neuhoff Packing Company. The radio announcer didn't give any clues as to the identity of the robbers, except that they had made a clean escape from the crime scene.

Clyde and Raymond, who were flush with the proceeds of their latest venture, subsequently picked up Bonnie. The two thieves drove Bonnie to their hideout in Grand Prairie. A few days later, Clyde and Raymond dropped Bonnie back with her mother. Then, the two men drove across the state border, into Oklahoma. This showed basic criminal cunning on Clyde's part. Robbery was a state crime. If a robbery were committed in one state, police were not allowed to pursue the suspects if they crossed the border into another state. Until Clyde violated a federal law (murder wasn't a federal offense at the time), he could keep zipping across state lines to evade arrest.

NOTES

1. L. J. "Boots" Hinton, interview with author, November 17, 2006.

2. Ibid.

3. As with just about every other major player in the Bonnie and Clyde saga, there exists a Web site dedicated to telling the story of Blanche Barrow's life. The site www.dazzled.com/blanche contains excellent photographs of the young Blanche.

4. For more information, see Piers Brendon, *The Dark Valley: A Panorama of the 1930s* (London: Jonathan Cape, 2000).

5. Ibid., p. 75.

6. Bonnie Parker's poetry is published in a number of sources and is also widely available online at http://texashideout.tripod.com/bc.htm. This site offers an entire section devoted to Bonnie's literary musings.

7. Another account states that Clyde purchased gasoline, not guitar strings, from Bucher.

Chapter 3

ALONG FOR THE RIDE

Three men sat in a stolen car, drinking and laughing. Clyde usually didn't imbibe, but he was feeling unusually expansive that warm, summer night. As the bottle went around, he drank heartily. Raymond Hamilton was in the car with him, along with a friend of his, identified as Everett Milligan (some accounts say this was an alias, and that the man's real name as Ross Dyer). The trio guzzled bootleg whisky and swapped crime stories. As with any journey involving Clyde, the car was filled with guns.

It was early August, and Clyde was behind the wheel, as always. They were driving aimlessly through southern Oklahoma. They had no real plan or destination in mind. Constant movement, however, seemed wise now that Clyde was wanted for murder. At some point, the men heard music and went to investigate.

The music was coming from an open-air country dance, held near Stringtown in Atoka County. Clyde drew the car closer for a better look. Inside a well-lit dance area, bordered by a banister, country gentlemen swung their ladies and stomped their boots. The ladies wore summer dresses, which rippled as they twirled. The music was provided by a quartet of teenagers playing a fiddle, banjo, and two guitars. There were no drums. The band played jigs and reels from the British Isles and old-fashioned country and folk music. Their voices and instruments carried over the countryside as they performed.

If he were sober, Clyde might have turned the car around and made tracks. Since the John Bucher killing, Clyde had been extra-alert and wary. There was no way he wanted to go back to Eastham. He kept a low profile and generally avoided any place where police might happen to be.

But Clyde was not sober, which was unusual for him. He was off his guard, and feeling relaxed. He doubted any police officers would be looking for him at a hick dance in Oklahoma. It didn't occur to him that a stolen vehicle packed with guns might stand out at a country party.

Clyde eased the car closer to the dance floor. The vehicle moved inside the circle of light around the dance area. Clyde stopped the engine, then tapped his hands on the steering wheel in time to the lively music. The whisky bottle went back and forth between the three men as they watched the proceedings on the dance floor.

At one point, Everett decided to get involved in the fun. He stepped out of the car and walked toward the dance. Clyde didn't stop him. What harm could Everett do? The police had no idea who he was. People probably came to the dance from miles around. There didn't seem much else to do on a hot summer night in the Oklahoma countryside. It's likely no one would even notice the addition of a stranger on the dance floor.

Clyde and Raymond sat and drank, oblivious to the attention they were drawing from unwanted quarters. A police officer named Sheriff Eugene Moore was eyeing the two men warily. He thought it odd that the pair would sit in their car and watch other people having fun. That seemed to be a strange thing to do, when no one was stopping them from joining in the dancing themselves. A third man from the car had just stepped onto the dance floor. Why didn't his buddies follow him?

The observant police officer also noticed Clyde and Raymond passing around what appeared to be a bottle. He doubted it was filled with Coca-Cola. Clyde and Raymond talked in loud voices and seemed drunk. Prohibition might have been a joke in the big cities, but it was still vigorously enforced in more rural parts of the country. The sheriff decided to get a closer look at the intruders.

As Sheriff Moore started walking to Clyde's car, another cop named Sheriff C. G. Maxwell joined him. The two lawmen drew near. When they were very close, they prepared to address the car's occupants, to find out their business. Instead, a barrage of gunfire greeted the two sheriffs.

Sheriff Maxwell was hit several times, in his torso and limbs. He fell to the ground as Sheriff Moore watched in wide-eyed astonishment. On the dance floor, Everett froze. The musicians stopped playing, their final notes trailing in the night air. Women screamed and their partners prepared to help the downed sheriff. A group of men rushed Clyde's car, a solid line of farm muscle, while another bunch ran toward the injured lawmen.

Clyde gunned the engine and raced across the grass. Dancers leapt out of his way while Sheriff Maxwell struggled to raise himself up on one elbow. As Clyde weaved and bobbed and tried to escape, Sheriff Maxwell drew his gun and fired at the departing vehicle. He was badly wounded, but determined to fight back. Sheriff Moore also drew his weapon, in preparation of getting a few shots off.

Clyde made it back to the road by which he had arrived, but didn't get too far. Thanks to the combination of alcohol and blind fear, his driving was erratic. He drove off the road and smashed the vehicle into a culvert. Clyde and Raymond snatched some guns, then leapt out of the totaled car. They stood for a moment, and fired several shots toward the brightly lit dance area.

Some of the male dancers had retrieved their own weapons by this point. The night air crackled with gunfire as the country gentlemen shot in the general direction of Clyde and Raymond. In all of the chaos, some of the dancers were hit by stray rounds and cried out. Sheriff Moore took a bullet in the chest and toppled over. The round had pierced his heart; he would soon be dead. Sheriff Maxwell survived, although badly injured. A partygoer picked up Moore's weapon and added to the barrage of lead aimed at Clyde and his partner.

Everett tried to run to rejoin his pals. A group of men tackled him and held him down, despite his protests. Clyde and Raymond made no effort to intervene and rescue their captured compatriot.

Clyde and Raymond stopped firing to collect as many bullets as they could grab from the car. Then they got down on all fours and crawled along the culvert, into darkness. The dancers cursed as the intruders slithered from view. Soon, Clyde and Raymond could no longer be seen in the black night.

Moving as fast as they could, the two men made their way to another road. Clyde looked up and saw a pair of headlights bearing down on him. The lights came to a sudden stop and a male voice called out, asking whether Clyde and Raymond needed help. They certainly did. Smiling at the stroke of good luck, Clyde stood up and waved his pistol in the Good Samaritan's face. He ordered the shocked driver to move over, then commandeered his vehicle. Clyde pushed the Good Samaritan to the passenger's seat and took the driver's position himself. The owner of the car sat in stark terror as Raymond jumped into the back seat.

This time, Clyde managed to drive for a good 15 minutes before getting into an accident. Once again, no one was hurt. Clyde and Raymond ditched the vehicle, and their petrified hostage, and made their way to a nearby farmhouse. They kept their weapons out of sight as they pounded on the door with their fists. The door opened to reveal a farmer. Clyde immediately launched into a story about a car accident. He said they had to take an injured party to the hospital right away, lest they die by the roadside.

The farmer seemed sympathetic. A relative of his who happened to be at the house said he would drive the men to the hospital. He asked Clyde where the accident had taken place, then walked out of the farmhouse and into his car, which was parked nearby. Clyde waited until the man turned on the ignition, then put his pistol against his temple. The man's mouth fell open in shock as Clyde ordered him to keep quiet and move over. For the second time in under an hour, Clyde commandeered a vehicle and took a hostage. With the frightened relative quaking in the passenger seat, Clyde and Raymond made their getaway.

Clyde drove to a township called Clayton. His senses were once again sharp and focused. The effects of the whisky seemed to have dissipated, with all the adrenaline that was rushing through him. Clyde kept a careful watch for police cars as he cruised the small township. In Clayton, Clyde stole yet another vehicle. He ditched the hostage and slinked back to Texas with Raymond.

The entire evening had been a pointless criminal endeavor. Clyde and Raymond probably could have talked their way out of trouble when the two sheriffs came by their vehicle. The cops, after all, merely thought they had some party crashers on their hands, not wanted fugitives. Sheriffs Moore and Maxwell were concerned that Clyde and Raymond appeared to be drinking. They had no clue the two men were heavily armed and ready to shoot.

Even if Clyde had pulled his gun, there was no reason he had to fire. A calmer criminal might have simply disarmed the officers and quietly driven away into the night. Or taken the sheriffs hostage to guarantee a safe getaway.

As it was, Clyde had left behind one dead sheriff, one badly wounded sheriff, two wrecked cars, and a crowd of terrorized dancers. A friend of one of his accomplices had been captured, and was more than likely going to talk. Clyde had also accomplished something else; thanks to the death of Sheriff Eugene Moore, Clyde could now add "cop killer" to his burgeoning criminal resume.

Shortly after the Stringtown shootings, Clyde sent a friend to pick up Bonnie at her mother's place. Bonnie was taken to the disused farmhouse in Grand Prairie that had been established as the gang's hideout. While at this hideout, Clyde made occasional forays into Dallas to visit his family. The latter still supported him, despite Clyde's continued descent into more serious crime.

While Clyde usually passed on highly edited or selective accounts of his adventures to his parents, he was quite candid about his exploits to other members of his clan. Clyde openly discussed the Stringtown incident with his sister Nell. He didn't deny shooting at the two lawmen. In his defense, Clyde pointed out that Raymond had fired too. Clyde said he didn't know which man actually killed Sheriff Moore.

In spite of this confession, Nell remained remarkably obtuse about her brother's true nature. She would soon become apt at making excuses for Clyde's criminal behavior. She blamed his antisocial attitude on his harsh treatment at Eastham. In fact, the whole Barrow family began to engage in a peculiar collective lie. They didn't turn Clyde in and even developed code words to announce his coming and goings. Cumie Barrow would let it be known she was "cooking red beans for dinner" whenever Clyde was planning on making a visit.

The police, by this point, were keeping a careful eye on Clyde's family. After being captured at the dance, Everett Milligan had told the cops everything he knew about Clyde. The police started a search for the ringleader of what they tagged "the Barrow Gang."

If the Barrow family overlooked Clyde's excesses, Bonnie openly embraced them. She stayed with her man, even after the killings of John Bucher and Sheriff Moore. If anything, she became closer to Clyde now that he was a murderer. There are many theories as to why Bonnie remained loyal to a felon. One school of thought suggests she was thrilled with Clyde's crimes. He offered danger, adventure, and daring, an appealing combination for a young woman whose life had been otherwise dull and unremarkable.

Bonnie was hardly the first young woman to become romantically involved with a homicidal psychopath. In the 1960s, Great Britain was shocked by the case of the "Moors Murderers"—a pair of killers who kidnapped, tortured, and murdered young children and buried them in the countryside. The Murderers were a male and female team, consisting of Myra Hindley and Ian Brady. Like Bonnie, Myra was a seemingly normal, intelligent young lady who fell in with an antisocial thug with extremely violent tendencies. When Ian suggested the two lovers start snatching children and murdering them, Myra went right along with it. The pair killed at least four people, probably more, by the time they were caught.[1]

Canada, likewise, was shocked by the horrid antics of another couple, Paul Bernardo and Karla Homolka, in the early 1990s. Karla was a bright teenager who started going out with Paul, knowing full well he was a rapist. Karla not only went along with her boyfriend's sexual proclivities, she offered up her younger sister as a drugged Christmas present for Paul. That teenage Tammy Homolka died after being doped by Karla and raped by Paul didn't stop the two lovebirds from tying the knot. Paul and Karla killed at least two more people—teenage girls who were kidnapped, tortured, and sexually abused. At the controversial trial that ensued, Karla testified against her husband as graphic details of their sordid life were exposed for all to see.

Bonnie's relationship with Clyde was odd, to say the least. Clyde wasn't affectionate and rarely kissed his sweetie. Apparently, he was also a bit of a dud in bed. Some lascivious histories go so far as to claim Clyde was gay and Bonnie an unfulfilled nymphomaniac. Whatever the case may be, Clyde seemed more interested in guns and cars than sex. Clyde and Bonnie both loved to get their picture taken, holding high-powered weapons in their hands.

If Clyde was somewhat of a failure as a thief, holdup artist, and lover, he did excel at driving. Now that he was on the road for much of the time, he was getting the hang of making fast getaways from tight situations. He also had a good memory for backcountry roads and off-the-map detours. Clyde thought nothing of driving for hours at a stretch, covering hundreds of miles in the process. "He believed in a non-stop jump in territory—sometimes as much as 1,000 miles—whenever it got hot behind," a member of the Barrow gang would later tell an interviewer.[2]

Clyde's driving skills came in handy, because the Barrow gang soon grew bored and uncomfortable at their Grand Prairie hideout. The August heat was unbearable, and there was a decided lack of creature comforts at the residence. A decision was made to drive to Carlsbad, a small community in New Mexico where an aunt of Bonnie's lived. Her name was Nettie Stamps, and she knew little of Bonnie's involvement in the criminal underworld.

Bonnie, Clyde, and Raymond Hamilton made the long journey to New Mexico. The trip was without incident, until a sheriff spotted them around Carlsbad. The lawman noted that Clyde was driving at high speed and had an out-of-state license plate. This was odd in an era where cross-country travel was rare (largely because gas was a luxury item in the Depression and the nation's highways were rough and primitive). The observant cop jotted down the plate number on Clyde's car. He then proceeded to run the number through highway department records and determined that the vehicle had been stolen. The officer began driving around, trying to relocate the stolen car. He finally found the vehicle parked at Nettie Stamps's residence.

The cop knocked at Nettie's door. When the door opened, the constable found himself staring down the barrel of a revolver, held in Clyde's hand. Clyde didn't kill the constable, he merely ordered him into his stolen vehicle. Bonnie and Raymond hopped in as well and the party took off. He drove for hundreds of miles with the unwitting passenger, until finally letting him off near San Antonio, Texas. The constable hadn't been physically harmed, although he was psychologically rattled. Clyde found the incident extremely amusing. Holding the power of life and death over another human being appealed to him. Humiliating a policeman also seemed a good way to strike back at "the law."

Once they had gotten rid of their prey, Clyde and Raymond stole two new vehicles—a Ford V-8 sedan and a Ford coupe. Clyde drove the coupe while Hamilton drove the sedan.

The choice of a Ford was no accident. Clyde was particularly partial to Ford V-8s, a rugged car capable of very high speeds. Ford V-8s had a comfy interior (an important matter for a gang on the run) and handled well. Clyde could turn the car on tight corners at top speed without losing control. The back seats of the four-door Ford V-8s had plentiful legroom (good for stretching out or stockpiling weapons). Finally, V-8s offered a relatively quiet ride and had good ventilation, which was a blessing in the scorching summer heat. Police departments of the day usually were equipped with far inferior six-cylinder cars. Clyde could race circles around most police vehicles.

"Clyde really banked on them Fords," a Barrow gang member later related in an interview. "They was the fastest and the best and he knew how to drive them with one foot in the gas tank all the time."[3]

It was a good thing Clyde picked such capable cars. After being alerted to the Barrow gang's presence, police went about establishing a trap for Clyde and company. They guessed (correctly as it turned out) that Clyde would be heading north, toward Houston. With this in mind, police set up an ambush near the Colorado River in a small Texas community called Wharton. The police planned to lure Clyde into the middle of the bridge that spanned the river. They would let him drive onto the bridge from the eastern side, then attack from the west once he was halfway across. It would difficult for even a good driver like Clyde to turn around on the narrow confines of the bridge. The police could then extract revenge for the death of Sheriff Moore.

The police expected the Barrow gang to be traveling in one car. They were surprised then, when the gang showed up in two vehicles. By the time the police had figured out that Clyde and Raymond were driving different cars, it was too late. Clyde spotted the police presence on the western side of the bridge and began furiously turning the steering wheel on his car. Just a few feet away from the bridge, Clyde swerved in a dramatic circle and started heading the opposite way down the road at high speed. Seeing what Clyde was doing, Raymond also pivoted and turned his back bumper to the cops. The police opened fire but none of their shots hit home. The two vehicles disappeared into the dust cloud kicked up by their spinning tires. Not for the last time, Clyde had eluded his would-be captors through the strength of his driving.

Shortly after their brief sojourn in New Mexico, the Barrow gang made another long-distance journey. Raymond Hamilton was eager to see his father in Bay City, Michigan. He mused about living with his dad and dropping out of the Barrow gang.

Clyde wasn't upset to hear this. His relationship with Raymond was starting to fray. Clyde disliked Raymond's extroverted, chatty nature. Raymond, in turn, thought Clyde was unwilling to tackle "big scores" in large cities. Raymond wanted to hit up big-city banks, rather than steal cars and rob from country grocers. So, on September 1, 1932, Bonnie and Clyde and Raymond made the 1,000-mile trip to Michigan. Clyde dropped his accomplice off at his father's house, and then headed back to Texas.

Clyde managed to stay out of trouble for about a month and a half. On October 11, 1932, Clyde made his presence felt again. Bonnie and Clyde were driving around the Texas countryside when they entered a small town called Sherman. Sherman was located roughly 45 miles to the north of Dallas. The pair spotted a general store and decided on the spur of the moment to rob it. Perhaps Clyde wanted to give Bonnie some experience in stickups. Or maybe they were just low on cash. For Clyde, robbery was like a normal 9-to-5 job. Whenever you needed money, you went out and committed a new robbery. It beat waiting around for a paycheck.

There are different takes on what happened next at the general store in Sherman. One account states that Bonnie entered the store with Clyde. She bought some bread and a can of salmon and presented the cashier with a five-dollar bill. When the cashier tried to give Bonnie her change, she pulled a pistol on him. Evidently, Clyde had been teaching her how to shoot and wanted to break her in, so to speak, to the criminal life.

Another version of the Sherman robbery depicts Bonnie as the getaway driver. In this telling, Clyde entered the store alone while Bonnie waited behind the wheel of their latest stolen vehicle. Clyde requested some cold cuts, then pulled out a gun and ordered the cashier to give up the till.

The storekeeper was a one-time cowboy named Howard Hall (some historians give the name as Hill or Hull). In any case, Hall wasn't about to let Clyde get away with robbing his business. Seeing Clyde point a gun at the store clerk, Hall grabbed a meat cleaver and raised it behind his head. Meat cleaver in hand, Hall rushed toward the intruder, who spun around at the last minute and fired his gun. The storekeeper stopped in his tracks, a bullet in his chest. He collapsed on the floor in front of his horrified cashier. The meat cleaver also hit the floor, where it lay, untouched.

Staring down in sheer terror at the dying Hall, the other store employees let Clyde have free run of the till. Clyde grabbed about $30, plus some groceries, and rushed out of the store. He took off with Bonnie as the shop clerks tried to recover from their shock. The store employees comforted Hall as best they could. They picked up their badly wounded co-worker and gingerly carried him to a nearby hospital. For all their efforts, Hall soon died from his injury.

For some reason, Clyde never liked to discuss the fatal robbery in Sherman. While he was happy to talk about gunning down cops, Clyde wouldn't even admit to being in Sherman, much less robbing a general store. Fingerprints inside Hall's shop gave away his presence, however. Clyde's denial probably had something to do with his self-image. Clyde liked to think of himself as a tough guy who shot it out with policemen and lived by his wits and cunning. Killing a storekeeper in cold blood—all for 30 bucks and some food items—seemed like the act of a panicky weakling, not a hard-boiled holdup man.

In the days after the Sherman killing, Clyde had other worries as well. Bonnie was going through an acute case of homesickness. She begged Clyde to drive back to Dallas so she could see her mother. Clyde eventually gave in, and plotted a clandestine return to Bonnie's hometown.

Clyde announced his arrival in town in a unique fashion. He wrote a note that he placed in a bottle, which was then tossed onto Cumie Barrow's lawn. The note contained specific instructions on where and when to meet. The Barrows in turn passed this information on to Bonnie's family. When it came time for the reunion, however, Henry and Cumie Barrow were there, but not Emma Parker. Mrs. Parker happened to be working and wasn't able to attend.

Bonnie sulked and whined. It wasn't fair that Clyde got to see his parents, when Bonnie couldn't see her mother. Once again, Clyde gave in. Family was family, after all. Clyde arranged for Bonnie to make a lighting-fast visit at the Parker household. As Bonnie dashed inside to see her mother, Clyde drove around the block, keeping a wary eye out for cops. Bonnie tearfully hugged and kissed her mom and assured her that everything was fine. Within a matter of minutes, Bonnie was back out of the door and into Clyde's car. The pair drove off, with no indication of when they planned a return visit.

Back in Bay City, Michigan, Raymond Hamilton was having a good time. Ever a congenial sort, Raymond was attracted to a young, pretty waitress in an eatery he frequented. To impress the girl, Raymond boasted of his connection with various criminals. He might have even mentioned Clyde Barrow by name. The girl thought Raymond had an interesting choice of friends. She contacted a policeman who happened to be pals with her and tipped him off about Raymond's criminal acquaintances.

On December 6, 1932, Raymond and the waitress went out on a date. The pair went roller-skating. They traded their street shoes for roller skates, then went sweeping across the skating rink. Their fun was interrupted by the arrival of several policemen. A rather awkward arrest ensued, given that Raymond was still wearing skates. Needless to say, Raymond did not attempt to make a run for it. He was taken into custody.

Bonnie and Clyde had a considerably better time of it that December. They arranged secret Christmas meetings with their families in Dallas and cast about for a replacement for Raymond Hamilton. Clyde felt it was necessary to get a partner who could help with heists and getaways. It seemed almost providential when Clyde found just such a person, in the form of a boy who used to hero-worship him back in the rough camp at the Houston Street Viaduct.

NOTES

1. For an excellent account of Myra Hindley and other female criminals, see Jay Robert Nash, *Look for the Woman: A Narrative Encyclopedia of Female Poisoners, Kidnappers, Thieves, Extortionists, Terrorists, Swindlers and Spies from Elizabethan Times to the Present* (London: Harrap, 1981).

2. W. D. Jones, "Riding with Bonnie and Clyde," *Playboy*, November 1968. The interview is posted online at http://www.cinetropic.com/janeloisemorris/commentary/bonn%26clyde/wdjones.html.

3. Ibid.

Chapter 4

ARMED FOR WAR

William Daniel Jones was short, tough, and impressionable. W. D., as he was commonly known, was born May 12, 1916, into a large, poor family in East Texas. His father, Jim Jones, was a sharecropper who moved the family into Dallas when W. D. was still a little boy. There, Jim took work in an iron plant.

Like the Barrows, the Jones family lived under the Houston Street Viaduct for a time. It was under the viaduct that little W. D. first met, and came to admire, a pubescent delinquent named Clyde Barrow. As soon as Jim could afford it, he arranged for his family to live in a real house in Dallas proper. In late January 1923, Jim died of influenza, along with W. D.'s teenage sister and brother. Mrs. Jones did the best she could to raise what was left of the family.[1]

W. D. claimed to have dropped out of school after the first grade, and as a result, never learned how to read. This didn't stop him from selling newspapers in downtown Dallas as a young boy. W. D. would ask passersby to read the headlines to him. Once he had a grasp on the headline, he'd start shouting it out loud to entice people to buy papers.

At age 11, W. D. had a brush with the law. He was accused of stealing a bicycle, but managed to talk his way out of trouble. W. D. remained close to the Barrow family. As an adolescent, he was friends with L. C. Barrow—one of Clyde's brothers. He continued to admire Clyde as well. "Clyde run with my older brother and he used to come calling on a girl who boarded at my house," W. D. later told *Playboy* magazine. "He went with her before Bonnie…I was just a kid, but Clyde always treated me nice and I liked him."[2]

As a teenager, W. D. was physically unimpressive. He stood around five feet six and had coarse features. He parted his dark hair down the middle and had a stolid, nondescript appearance. W. D. remained eager-to-please, however, and something of a hero-worshipper.

W. D. would later give police a long confession detailing his association with Bonnie and Clyde. He would also offer a lengthy interview with *Playboy* magazine in the late 1960s, following a renewal of interest in the outlaw couple. His police confession and *Playboy* interview differ on a few details but both feature a somewhat awestruck depiction of Clyde.

In *Playboy*, W. D. described his reunion with Clyde, on Christmas Eve, 1932: "Me and L. C.—that's Clyde's younger brother—was driving home from a dance in his daddy's old car. Here come Bonnie and Clyde. They honked their car horn and we pulled over. I stayed in the car. L. C. got out and went back to see what they wanted. And he hollered at me, 'Hey, come on back. Clyde wants to talk to you.' Clyde was wanted then for murder and kidnapping but I had knowed him all my life. So I got out and went to his car."[3]

Clyde announced that he was in town to visit his mother and Marie—his younger sister. He asked W. D. to stick around while L. C. fetched the two women. Clyde kept referring to W. D. as "boy"—an ironic tag, given that he was only seven years older than his viaduct comrade. W. D. didn't seem to mind; he was delighted to be in the famous outlaw's presence.

Clyde had his little family visit. After it was over, he didn't want W. D. to leave. Clyde told the teen that he and Bonnie had been cooped up in their car for a long time. They needed to get some sleep. Would W. D. accompany them, as they scouted out a safe location to catch some rest? W. D. didn't have to be asked twice. Although he was aware that associating with criminals could put his own freedom and safety in jeopardy, he went along with Clyde's request. W. D. was proud that Clyde trusted him so much. He figured it was because Clyde had known him from their poor childhood under the Houston Street Viaduct.

Around 2:00 A.M. on Christmas Day, the fatigued outlaws drove into a tourist camp near Temple, Texas. They booked a room and bedded down for the night. Bonnie and Clyde took over the bed while W. D. slept on the floor. The next morning, instead of opening presents or going to church, Clyde decided it was time to commit a robbery. He had W. D. change two tires on his car, then took the teenager along for a ride. Clyde drove around Temple, scouting out potential targets.

It was at this point, claimed W. D., that Clyde made him an active partner in crime. Clyde apparently handed W. D. a pistol—W. D. described it as an "old, .41 caliber thumb buster" in his *Playboy* interview and an "old .45 caliber single-action pistol" in his confession to police. Clyde informed the surprised teenager he had his eye on a grocery store. "Clyde told me that 'we' were going to hold up that store," W. D. stated in his police confession. "I didn't want to do it, but he insisted that I go in with him."[4]

Here, W. D.'s recollections are contradictory: In *Playboy*, W. D. said he "stood watch outside the store while Clyde went in." He offered a different story to the police: "We parked around the corner from the store and Clyde Barrow and I got out and went into the store. Bonnie Parker stayed in the car."

Clyde was armed with a .45 caliber pistol and a "16 gauge automatic shotgun with a sawed off barrel, strapped to his body and concealed under his overcoat," said W. D. in his police confession. "When we got into the store, Clyde made some small purchases and I believe we bought some eggs and some bread."

At this point, W. D. told police he "got worried and scared" and refused to go along with the stickup. He said he walked out of the store and into the erstwhile getaway car. Clyde followed him and "raised hell" because he wouldn't participate in the robbery. W. D. was considerably more vague in *Playboy* as to what transpired in the store, other than that Clyde "got the money" and the two walked out together.[5]

While either driving around Temple or walking back to Bonnie in the getaway car, Clyde spotted a vehicle he liked. It was a Model A Ford Roadster and Clyde figured it was just the thing to steal. He ordered W. D. to "hotwire" the vehicle and get it running.

W. D. did as he was told. He hopped inside the Ford Roadster and tried to get the motor started. To the teenager's consternation, the engine wouldn't turn over. The cold weather had made the motor sluggish and unresponsive. Flustered, W. D. surrendered the driver's seat to an impatient Clyde. As Clyde now tried to start the car, an elderly man and woman rushed out of a nearby house. They began yelling in union at Clyde and W. D. At this point, "another, younger man came out of the house and came up to the car on the side where Clyde was sitting," W. D. told police.[6]

The "younger man" was named Doyle Johnson. The roadster was his. The "older man" identified by W. D. was Henry Krauser, Johnson's father-in-law. Doyle's in-laws had been inside his house, celebrating Christmas. A young salesman, Doyle was married, with a baby daughter. He had been napping when Clyde and W. D. broke into his car.

W. D. told *Playboy* that Doyle physically reached inside the vehicle and started choking Clyde. He made no mention of this detail in his police confession. In either case, Clyde reacted violently to the young man's

presence.[7] "Clyde raised his pistol and fired at this man three times,"
W. D. told police, adding that he didn't see him fall. Doyle was killed, in
front of his house and before the eyes of his family. At this point, Clyde
and W. D. raced away in the stolen Ford Roadster. They connected with
Bonnie, then made a fast exit from town.

"We drove out of Temple and nearly drove to Waco, traveling on small
country roads and avoiding the highways," W. D. told police. "We parked
on a little country road most of the day and then went on at night, turning
off to the east before reaching Waco and avoiding towns as much as possible. Late that night we went into a tourist camp but I don't know where
it was. We stayed there until the next morning."[8]

Clyde allegedly told W. D. that he had no choice but to stay remain
with him and Bonnie. "'You can't go home,'" W. D. quotes Clyde as saying,
in *Playboy*. "'You got murder on you, just like me. You can't go home.'"[9]

It's questionable whether Clyde actually uttered these dramatic words.
However, W. D. did feel criminally bound to his childhood idol. If W. D.
had contemplated the matter a little more carefully, he might not have
been so eager to cleave to Clyde. The killing in Temple had been another
totally pointless murder. Clyde gained nothing from the killing (Doyle's
car was dumped shortly after Clyde and W. D. stole it) except for a growing
rep as a trigger-happy hood. The murder of an innocent man on Christmas Day was so distasteful that even Bonnie and Clyde's families were
appalled. Emma Parker would later falsely claim that the Doyle Johnson
killing took place in early December.

W. D. didn't have to wait long for Clyde to strike again. After hiding
out in tourist camps for a few days, Bonnie, Clyde, and W. D. drove back
into Dallas in early January 1933. It was the dawn of a new, momentous
year. Later that month, Adolf Hitler would be appointed Chancellor of
Germany—the first stepping-stone to total dictatorship. Hitler would
soon introduce a rearmament program aimed at making Germany the
most powerful nation in Europe. Alongside guns, Hitler also opened con-
centration camps for anyone who didn't fit the Nazi ideal—including
Jews, gypsies, the handicapped, and other minorities. In March, a new
president with the patrician name of Franklin Delano Roosevelt (FDR)
would take the oath of office in the United States. The country by this
stage was in desperate shape. "During the first two months of 1933, nearly
400 banks failed as depositors withdrew their funds and succumbed to
'hoarding mania'," states a history of the era.[10]

FDR would proceed to launch a dizzying array of government initiatives aimed at reversing or at least ameliorating the worst effects of the
Depression. While the programs produced mixed results, Roosevelt firmly

established the notion that government had a responsibility to help the poor.[11]

Big changes were also afoot in Dallas law-enforcement circles. Late in 1932, R. A. ("Smoot") Schmid was elected sheriff of Dallas County. A tough, forceful man, Sheriff Schmid was determined to make the police under his command more effective and professional. The sheriff hired dozens of new deputies who shared his two-fisted notion of law enforcement. One of his hires was a deputy named Ted Hinton who hailed from West Dallas. Not quite 30, Hinton was familiar with both Bonnie and Clyde. He had known the Barrow clan while growing up and had frequented one of the cafés where Bonnie worked as a waitress. His firsthand experience with the ringleaders of the Barrow gang made him indispensable to Sheriff Schmid.

In early 1933, the sheriff made another prominent hire by adding a deputy named Bob Alcorn to his ranks. An excellent rifleman, Deputy Alcorn would prove a great asset to Dallas law enforcement. Sheriff Schmid was determined to bring Bonnie and Clyde to justice. The opportunity to do just that would come sooner than the sheriff expected.

Dallas police had been tipped off that Clyde might try to visit an underworld buddy of his named Odell Chambless at the home of one Lillian McBride. The tip came the previous year from a bank robber who offered this information in the hopes of getting a reduced sentence. Lillian was Raymond Hamilton's sister and she lived in West Dallas. It was not unthinkable that Lillian might play host to a meeting between Clyde and one of his criminal associates.

Going on this vague tip, a small group of policemen, led by Sheriff Fred Bradberry, paid a visit to Lillian's residence. The sheriff was accompanied by a handful of lawmen, including Deputy Malcom Davis. The cops arrived on the evening of January 6, 1933, only to discover that Lillian wasn't home. Her older sister was present, however, and agreed to let the men inside the house. The sister said Lillian was off visiting her imprisoned brother. The police decided to stick around to see if she showed up. Some of the lawmen waited inside, while others waited outside.

The police asked Lillian's sister to turn off the house lights. She agreed, provided she could keep a nightlight on in a room occupied by her small son. The lawmen acceded to this request and all the lights—bar the one in the child's bedroom—were doused.

Around midnight, police heard a car driving up to the house. The car approached, then revved off. Sheriff Bradberry prepared his men. Sure enough, the car returned. The lawmen counted three people inside the vehicle, two men and a woman. Perhaps this was Lillian, returned with some friends. The police were stunned when they realized one of the three was none other than Clyde Barrow.

The tipster had been right; as W. D. Jones related in his confession to police, "Clyde was trying to get some information about Raymond" from his sister. W. D. wasn't clear as to what information Clyde was seeking. Odell Chambless didn't appear to play a role in this intelligence-gathering mission, given that he wasn't home when Clyde came calling.

Clyde stepped out of the vehicle as the lawmen waited and fingered their weapons. He walked up to the door of the house and knocked. Inside, Sheriff Bradberry whispered to Lillian's sister to let Clyde in. There is some confusion over what happened next. Some reports state that Lillian's sister opened the door but tipped off Clyde about the police presence. She might have been afraid a gunfight would erupt, putting her son at risk. Another take has it that Clyde somehow sensed the police and grabbed his gun.

"Clyde had a sawed-off 16 gauge automatic shotgun along with him all the time," stated W. D. in his *Playboy* interview. "It had a one-inch rubber band he'd cut out of a car-tire inner tube attached to the cut-off stock. He'd slip his arm through the band and when he put his coat on, you'd never know the gun was there. The rubber band would give when he snatched it up to fire. He kept his coat pocket cut out so he could hold the gun barrel next to his hip. It looked like he just had his hand in his pocket."[12]

Clyde used this shotgun to blast at Sheriff Bradberry, who was standing unobtrusively inside the darkened house. He missed. Outside the home, Deputy Davis heard the shotgun and raced around the corner to investigate. W. D. related what happened next in his police confession: "I saw two men come around the corner of Lillie McBride's house...then the shot rang out and Bonnie Parker told me to start the motor. I saw one of those two men fall and I began starting the motor. I don't know whether the two men fired or only one of them fired. I was so excited I didn't know how many shots they fired. Bonnie fired her pistol twice or three time, I am not sure which."[13]

This contradicts other testimony from W. D., to the extent that he never actually saw Bonnie shoot a weapon at anyone. In his *Playboy* interview, W. D. said, "As far as I know, Bonnie never packed a gun. Maybe she'd help carry what we had in the car into a tourist court...but during the big gun battles I was with them, she never fired a gun. But I'll say that she was a hell of a loader."[14]

Clyde pivoted on his feet and fired his weapon at Deputy Davis as he rounded the corner of the house. The blast hit the lawman at almost point-blank range. He flew backward as he absorbed the brutal force of the shotgun. The remaining police shouted at each other as they drew their weapons. Clyde dashed back to the car, firing all the while. He leapt in and took the wheel and raced off into the night. Back on Lillian McBride's lawn, police did what they could to comfort their critically wounded comrade. It was no use. Deputy Davis died of his injuries, becoming the fifth victim of the Barrow gang in the process.

In late January 1933, while motoring through Springfield, Missouri, Clyde had another close encounter with police. His driving drew the attention of Constable Thomas Persell, who was in a squad car. Constable Persell described what happened in a lengthy interview with the *Springfield (MO) Press*.

"A few minutes before 6 o'clock Thursday night, as I was cruising near the corner of Kimbrough Avenue and St. Louis Street, I noticed suspicious actions of three persons in a V-8 model Ford coach," said Persell. "A girl was riding in the front seat with two men and they looked as if they were trying to spot a car."

The constable had caught up with Clyde, Bonnie, and W. D. as they prowled the streets for a vehicle to steal. The constable watched the trio cruise around town. Persell waited until Clyde had driven onto the Benton Avenue Viaduct, then tried to intercept him.

"I pulled up beside the machine and ordered the driver to stop, but he declared that he didn't have any brakes," explained Persell in the *Press*. "At the end of the viaduct, he turned east on Pine Street and stopped. I noticed that the girl had got into the back seat of the car. Her arm was lying on the back of the seat and she had something in her hand. But I didn't know until later that it was a .45 army automatic."

"As I pulled up beside the machine, the driver stepped out with a sawed-off automatic shotgun in his hands and ordered me to hold up my hands and step into the car," continued the constable. "He jerked my gun out of my holster and threw it to his companion in the front seat."

Instead of murdering the lawman, Clyde thought it would be great fun to take him for a ride, so to speak. The car took off, with the constable sitting uncomfortably in the front seat with Clyde. It became apparent that Clyde had no clue where he was going. The master of back roads and country trails was lost in the confines of Springfield. Clyde was forced to ask his reluctant passenger for directions on how to get out of town. Constable Persell obliged and soon the car had left Springfield for new destinations. At one point, Clyde pulled over at a gas station to fuel up. As a precaution, the gang ordered Persell into the back seat and covered him with a blanket. Bonnie held a pistol on the lawman to keep him quiet. Once the vehicle was refueled, Persell was ordered to climb into the front passenger seat again.

While moving about inside the Ford, the constable noticed a large amount of cash, including "several sacks of coins" as well as an impressive collection of guns. The cop took the time to make some mental notes about his escorts. He said Clyde was the clear leader of the gang. He referred to Bonnie as "hon" or "babe" and relied on her map-reading skills for navigation. Persell described W. D. as "a silent sort of chap" who "addressed the girl as 'sis'." Bonnie called W. D. "bud" in return.

Persell had a pack of cigarettes on him. He smoked throughout his ordeal. Bonnie puffed cigs as well. When she ran low on tobacco, she sponged cigarettes from Persell. The lawman said Bonnie appeared to be a chain-smoker. Clyde, by contrast, didn't smoke at all. The kidnapped cop also noticed that the two men in the vehicle "seemed to have a mania for V-8 Fords."

Clyde rode around somewhat aimlessly. Fearing that his battery was dying, Clyde drove into a small town and stole a battery from a garage. He ordered the kidnapped lawman to help him remove the old battery from the engine and put in the freshly stolen battery. Once the battery was installed, Clyde took the wheel again.

"After throwing the old battery away, we turned the car around and drove about six or seven miles past some intersection," related the lawman. "The driver then said, 'Did you see that intersection?' And at an affirmative answer, he continued, 'We're going to dump you here. You walk to that intersection, turn right, and you'll come to a filling station and tourist camp. You can get a telephone there.' They let me out at 12:30. I looked at my watch. But when I asked for my gun, the driver refused and said, 'You're lucky as it is.' I walked about eight miles, but it seemed like a 100 before I got to the camp," continued Constable Persell. "There I called Joplin police, and they sent a car after me."[15]

Persell wasn't the only person to observe Bonnie and Clyde up close and personal during this period. W. D. also had plenty of opportunities to witness the ringleaders of the Barrow gang in action. For a "silent sort of chap," W. D. had plenty to say about his experiences with Bonnie and Clyde in later years.

Clyde almost always drove, because no one else would go as fast as he liked, W. D. recalled. Clyde liked Fords but he didn't get too attached to any of the vehicles he stole. The gang usually ditched their cars after a week or two. Keeping a stolen car any longer would be inviting trouble. Clyde made it a habit to always have a steady supply of stolen license plates on hand. After grabbing a car, Clyde would remove the plate and put on a different one to fool the police. Bonnie and Clyde's getaway vehicles were always packed with plates—as well as guns, food, and clothes.

Just as the gang didn't keep any of their cars for long, they didn't linger in any one locale for more than a few days or even hours. To keep their clothes clean, Clyde and Co. would drop off their duds at a dry-cleaners, then swing by a week or two later to retrieve them. Sometimes, they didn't pick up their clothes at all, preferring to buy new threads rather than risk exposure or capture by going back to the dry-cleaner.

Bonnie typically took care of shopping, for food and other supplies. W. D. and Clyde would wait for her in a car, guns within easy reach. They tried to keep out of sight as much as possible. Clyde, W. D. told *Playboy*, "always believed in being prepared"—which was a nice way of saying he was always ready to kill. W. D. also made clear that Clyde was "the complete boss" of the gang; he was respectful of Bonnie's wishes and desires but didn't let her order him about.[16]

Even if she wasn't the "complete boss," W. D. had good things to say about Bonnie. She was always neat and tidy, W. D. related to *Playboy*, her face covered in makeup and her hair combed, even while living on the road. Her fashion preferences ran toward long dresses and high heels. Clyde also took pride in his appearance and usually wore a suit, dress shoes, and a tie.

Bonnie and Clyde weren't the only outlaws of the period. The years 1933–1934 featured a crime wave unlike anything the United States had experienced before. In addition to the Barrow gang, criminals such as John Dillinger, Charles Arthur (aka "Pretty Boy Floyd"), George Barnes (aka "Machine Gun Kelly"), Lester Gillis (aka "Baby Face Nelson"), and the notorious Barker clan stalked the landscape.[17]

If these outlaws had anything in common, it was that most of them were more successful than the Barrow gang. While Clyde was content to knock off gas stations and grocery stores for petty cash, their contemporaries aimed for more rewarding targets. They robbed major banks in big cities or conducted lucrative kidnappings. The Barker family, for example, carried out abductions that brought in upward of $200,000. Bonnie and Clyde were not popular with their peers; John Dillinger considered the pair a bit of penny-ante thugs who gave holdup artists a bad name.

Outlaws of the 1930s benefited from fast cars, powerful guns, public sympathy, and substandard policing. In small or rural communities, the local police department was often made up of political appointees, not skilled constables. Communication between police branches was minimal.

Outside of the big cities, police departments were poorly staffed and badly funded.

Nor could local police rely on the federal government for much help. There practically was no federal police force to speak of at the time. At the dawn of the Depression, the Federal Bureau of Investigation (FBI) consisted of a few hundred underpaid agents. These agents weren't even allowed to carry guns or make arrests. They were supposed to perform "citizen's arrests" when apprehending suspects, or ask local police for help. The public was largely unfamiliar with the bureau and few criminals feared it.

The FBI had been launched in 1908, as a small division inside the Department of Justice. One year after its launch, the division acquired a name: it was called the Bureau of Investigation. The bureau's mandate was to investigate federal crimes, not state or local offenses. At the time, however, there were very few federal crimes on the books. The bureau had to content itself with investigating such things as bankruptcy, antitrust, land fraud, and naturalization violations. Violent crime, such as murder, was handled at a state or local level. The Mann Act of 1910 (which made it a federal offense to transport a woman across state lines for "immoral purposes") and the Motor Vehicle Theft Act of 1919 (which concerned cross-state car robbery) gave the bureau a little more clout, but not much.[18]

The bureau was renamed the United States Bureau of Investigation in 1932. A year later, it was merged with the Prohibition Bureau to become the Division of Investigation. It took more than a name change, however, to mold the organization into a professional police force. The catalyst in propelling the bureau into the front ranks of crime fighting was the notorious "Kansas City Massacre," which took place on June 17, 1933.

The main target of the massacre was Frank Nash, a murderer and bank robber with important criminal friends. Nash had been captured in Hot Springs, Arkansas, after escaping from Leavenworth Federal Prison in Kansas. He was placed under guard on a train in Fort Smith, Arkansas. His escorts consisted of two Division of Investigation agents and Police Chief Otto Reed of McAlester, Oklahoma.

Nash was taken off the train in Kansas City in order to be shipped back to Leavenworth. Special Agent Raymond Caffrey and an official named Reed Vetterli, both from the bureau, met the prisoner and his escorts. A pair of local police detectives accompanied Caffrey and Vetterli. Surrounded by peace officers and federal agents, Reed was hustled through the train station and into a parking lot. He was about to be placed in a car when several bursts of machine gunfire tore into the lawmen. Caffrey, the two local detectives, and Police Chief Reed were all killed. Nash himself was also gunned down. The killers were later identified as Vernon Miller, "Pretty Boy" Floyd, and Adam Richetti. It was never clear if the assassins were attempting to free or silence Nash.[19] This event shocked the public, and directly as a result of it, Division of Investigation agents were granted the right to make arrests and carry guns in June 1934. One year later, the organization changed its name a final time, to the Federal Bureau of Investigation.

As headed by J. Edgar Hoover (an extremely capable bureaucrat who took over the bureau in 1924), the FBI fought a public relations battle for respect. As Hoover realized, a large segment of the public sympathized with the very outlaws the FBI was trying to stamp out. After the disaster of Prohibition, which saw police ineffectually trying to enforce a federal ban on booze, people were cynical about law enforcement. The Great Depression made the situation worse. In an era of bank foreclosures and mass unemployment, gun-toting outlaws were seen by many as heroes fighting back against a tyrannical government.

Outlaws of the 1930s enjoyed another major advantage over their police counterparts in the form of weaponry. As the Kansas City Massacre brutally demonstrated, machine guns more than leveled the playing field for crooks. Hoods no longer had to be proficient at target practice to make an impression on police. Even the most inexperienced thug could operate a Tommy gun.

Machine guns weren't new. They had been around since the late nineteenth century and were responsible for much of the carnage of the First World War. Machine guns used by the military weren't conducive to committing crimes, however. They were heavy and required a two-man crew to operate. One soldier fed an ammunition belt into the weapon while another did the actual firing. They were far too bulky to employ for bank robberies. It took a government employee named General John Thompson to turn the machine gun into something any ordinary crook could use. General Thompson oversaw U.S. Army efforts to create a handheld machine gun. The army ended up producing a weapon called the Thompson submachine gun. The Tommy gun, as it was nicknamed, went into mass production in the early 1920s.

General Thompson described his invention as a "trench broom"—a weapon that individual soldiers could use to sweep aside enemies in close-quarter combat. To this end, the Tommy gun was relatively compact: It measured 33 inches in length and weighed around 11 pounds, unloaded. While small, the Thompson submachine gun packed a lethal punch. It could fire 600–800 rounds of .45 caliber bullets a minute. The weapon came equipped with a 20–30 bullet detachable box magazine or a 50–100 round drum magazine.[20]

Initially, the army didn't care much for the Thompson. It used up too much costly ammunition for one thing. Criminals were quicker to realize the fantastic potential of the weapon. Tommy guns became prized items on the black market. They helped turned Prohibition-era Chicago into a slaughterhouse, as gangs battled for control of the alcohol trade.

The Thompson submachine gun gave criminals an enormous edge. Most police departments outside large cities had nothing more powerful than .38 caliber revolvers and shotguns in their arsenals. Suddenly, they were faced with criminals whose firepower was the equivalent of a squad of riflemen. John Dillinger loved the Thompson machine gun, and so did Machine Gun Kelly (who acquired his nickname thanks to his association with the weapon). Combined with fast cars, machine-gun–toting criminals could zip around the country, robbing banks and terrorizing outgunned police.

Clyde Barrow appreciated the Thompson, but he favored an even more lethal weapon of the period: the Browning Automatic Rifle (BAR). Invented in 1917 by weapons designer John Browning, the BAR was deadly, if difficult to use. It resembled an ordinary rifle with a bulky box magazine. This box magazine could fire large-size .30–06 rifle rounds at the rate of 300–650 shots a minute. An experienced handler could unload the BAR's 20-round magazine in under three seconds. A round from a BAR could penetrate body armor and the metal plating on most cars. Like the Thompson, the Browning Automatic Rifle was intended for military use.

The BAR was heavy, weighing almost twice as much as a Thompson. At nearly 50 inches long, it was awkward to operate. It was, however, deadlier than a Tommy gun. In addition to firing a much bigger cartridge, the BAR had superior range; a Thompson submachine gun wasn't much good after 50 yards. A Browning Automatic Rifle, by contrast, could still hit targets at 600 yards.[21]

Constable Persell reported seeing both a Thompson submachine gun and a BAR in the stolen vehicle Clyde drove around Springfield. "I saw a veritable arsenal, bigger than the one at the police station on the floor of the car when I climbed over," Persell told the *Press*. "There were two rifles, two automatic shotguns, a Thompson submachine gun and a lot of pistols, including mine."[22]

Clyde was more lethal than ever before. As Persell observed, the hick from the Houston Street Viaduct was now armed for war with military-grade weapons.

NOTES

1. "Father and Child Die of Pneumonia," *Dallas Times Herald,* January 28, 1923.

2. W. D. Jones, "Riding with Bonnie and Clyde," *Playboy,* November 1968.

3. Ibid.

4. Ibid.

5. W. D. Jones's confession to police was made November 18, 1933, at the Dallas County Sheriff's Office in Dallas, Texas.

6. Ibid.

7. Jones, *Playboy.*

8. Jones, police confession.

9. Jones, *Playboy.*

10. Piers Brendon, *The Dark Valley: A Panorama of the 1930s* (London: Jonathan Cape, 2000), p. 87.

11. For a good description of FDR and the New Deal, see Conrad Black, *Franklin Delano Roosevelt* (New York: Public Affairs, 2005).

12. Jones, *Playboy.*

13. Jones, police confession.

14. Jones, *Playboy.*

15. Constable Thomas Persell was interviewed at length by Perry Smith of the *Springfield (MO) Press* on January 27, 1933. Like many Bonnie and Clyde–related articles and documents, the full transcript of the interview can be seen online at http://texashideout. tripid.com/bc.htm

16. Jones, *Playboy.*

17. See Bryan Burrough, *Public Enemies: America's Greatest Crime Wave and the Birth of the FBI, 1933–1934* (New York: Penguin Books, 2004) for a highly detailed account of Depression-era outlaws. See Stone Wallace, *Dustbowl Desperadoes: Gangsters of the Dirty '30s* (Edmonton, Alb.: Folk Lore Publishing, 2003) for a more concise view.

18. See www.fbi.gov, the FBI's official Web site. See Michael Newton, *The FBI Encyclopedia* (Jefferson, N.C.: McFarland & Company, 2003), for a more objective account of the agency's operations and history.

19. The FBI's Web site, www.fbi.gov, and *The FBI Encyclopedia* both contain detailed descriptions of the Kansas City Massacre. The massacre was either a bloody debacle or a great success for the underworld. If the aim was to rescue Nash, then the massacre was a disaster. If the aim was to silence Nash—by killing him—then the massacre was a success.

20. For a fascinating look at the history and mechanics of the Thompson submachine gun, see www.auto-ordnance.com.

21. Wikipedia.org contains a detailed description of the BAR, along with photos and external links.

22. Persell, *Springfield Press.*

Chapter 5

BLOOD BROTHERS

Buck Barrow was a free man, but his wife wasn't celebrating. In fact, Blanche Barrow was a nervous wreck. Buck had been released from Texas State Prison at Huntsville, thanks to a strenuous lobbying campaign waged by Blanche and Cumie Barrow. Both women were able to convince authorities that Buck had reformed. They pointed out that Buck had voluntarily surrendered. On top of that, Buck had been a model prisoner during his time at Huntsville, who gave every indication he wanted to go straight. Buck received a pardon from Texas governor Miriam "Ma" Ferguson in late March 1933. Blanche still worried, however. While her man said and did all the right things, she wondered if his will was strong enough to resist the temptation of a life of crime.

Aside from being slight, Buck didn't look much his younger brother. A wanted poster circulated later that year pegged Buck at five feet five and 110 pounds. He had chestnut-colored hair and a ruddy, outdoorsy complexion. While Clyde had delicate features, Buck looked like a hardened field hand. More significant, he completely lacked Clyde's charisma and drive. He was quiet and passive.[1]

With money from family members, Buck bought a Ford sedan. He hoped to use the vehicle to visit his in-laws. Blanche's family lived on a farm in Missouri (some sources say Oklahoma). Buck even toyed with the idea of working on the farm—an unlikely proposition given he hated manual labor as much as Clyde.

There was a fly in the ointment, however; Buck wanted to see his outlaw brother. That Clyde was a wanted man and a cop-killer didn't dissuade Buck. Using their sister Nell Cowan as an intermediary, Buck and Clyde passed a series of messages back and forth. The brothers decided to meet up near Fort Smith, Arkansas, along with their respective partners and accomplices. After everyone got acquainted, they would all travel to Joplin, Missouri, for some fun and relaxation. Joplin was chosen because it was known to be a haven for criminals and gangsters at the time. Its police force and politicians were notoriously corrupt.

Blanche cried and pleaded but Buck was adamant. He wanted to visit his brother. Perhaps he could convert Clyde to the righteous path and convince him to give up, much as Blanche had persuaded Buck to surrender. Together with his high-strung wife, Buck traveled to Fort Smith, to await Clyde, Bonnie, and W. D.

Buck and Clyde had a joyous reunion, then the expanded crew drove to Joplin, as planned. Clyde had already selected a hideout. He had previously rented an apartment at the back of a house located at 34th Street and Oakridge Drive. For the purpose of renting the space, Clyde claimed to be a civil engineer named Callaghan.

The rental unit was quite expansive; it had two bedrooms, a living room, a bathroom, and a kitchen. A double-garage was situated directly underneath the apartment. This suited Clyde just fine. He could use the garage to hide any cars he stole. It would also be handy for making a getaway, if need be.

For about two weeks, all went well. Clyde and Buck were delighted to be back in each other's company. They swapped stories about life in prison and in the criminal world. Blanche annoyed everyone with her high-strung nature, but Bonnie and Clyde put up with her for the sake of family unity. The group largely spent their days behind drawn curtains. They gossiped, read magazines, slept, and generally took it easy.

Neighbors in the area were starting to get concerned, however. They found it odd that the five people at 34th Street rarely went outside during the daytime. When they did appear in public, they were often spotted carrying guns of various sorts. Neighbors also wondered about the large number of license plates the group kept hauling into the apartment.

The nosey neighbors contacted the police, who in turn, sent over some highway patrolmen to keep an eye on the apartment. Police observed the apartment for three days. They became convinced that a bunch of bootleggers or local crooks were holed up in the place. Joplin P. D. decided a raid was in order. Apparently, Joplin wasn't quite as amenable to criminals as Clyde thought it was.

Around 4:00 P.M. on April 13, 1933, the police showed up in force. Inside the apartment, Bonnie was cooking dinner, while Blanche played cards and Buck napped. Outside, two police cars suddenly appeared in front of the apartment. As they approached, the cops spotted someone—most likely Clyde—by the garage doors. An officer barked an order. He told one of the constables to run inside the garage before the door slammed shut. Constable Wesley Harryman obediently jumped out of the vehicle and trotted over to the garage. At that moment, Clyde came into view inside the garage, shotgun in hand. Clyde fired and the unfortunate constable was ripped apart.

According to legend, Clyde yelled, "It's the law!" to his companions. Inside the apartment, everyone reacted immediately. W. D., and possibly Bonnie, opened fire from the upstairs windows with a pair of Browning Automatic Rifles. The windows shattered from the impact of the bullets. The police took cover behind their vehicles as the outlaws sprayed the property with lethal BAR fire. When they recovered from their shock, the cops drew their own weapons and fired back. The police were not well armed; they thought they would be busting minor-league bootleggers that day, not the Barrow gang. The peace officers did what they could, however, and peppered the apartment with small-arms fire. In a flash, the residence was filled with flying bullets and debris.

Blanche began screaming hysterically. She rushed out of the building and onto the street, shrieking her head off. The police were so amazed they held their fire, and Blanche got away unscathed.

Bolting from behind a car, Detective Harry McGinnis tried to rush the garage. Clyde fired another blast from his shotgun, maiming the lawman. The cop's arm was blown clear off. Detective McGinnis staggered in shock and collapsed, twitching and bleeding.

With one comrade dead and another horribly wounded, the three policemen remaining tried to determine a plan of action. One cop rushed around to the back of the apartment to find an alternative entrance. Another constable raced to a nearby house to call for backup. This left only a single peace officer at the crime scene, and he only had one bullet left in his pistol. While trying to reload, the lawman tripped and landed on his back. Clyde thought the man was shot. The cop was unhurt, however, and when W. D. appeared by the garage, the constable fired. W. D. was hit. Some crime historians say W. D. took a shot in the head. In his *Playboy* interview, W. D. located his injury farther south. "I got shot in the side at Joplin and my belly ached so bad I thought the bullet had stopped there," he told *Playboy*.[2]

While painful, W. D.'s wound wasn't critical, which was fortunate, as the Barrow gang had no time to tend to his injuries. Bonnie and Buck dived into one of the cars parked in the apartment's garage. Clyde jumped into the driver's seat and prepared to take off. At this point, an infuriated

Clyde realized one of the police cruisers was blocking his way. He stepped out of the vehicle and fired his shotgun at the remaining cop.

In spite of his injury, W. D. retained enough presence of mind to run to the police cruiser and release the parking brake. He pushed the car and it began to roll away. W. D. and Clyde might have also moved Constable Harryman's body while they were at it.

With the way now clear, Clyde leapt back into the driver's seat. W. D. took a spot in the back of the vehicle. As W. D. fired an automatic weapon—either a BAR or a Tommy gun—through the window, Clyde tore out of the garage and away from the apartment. Bonnie indicated the direction Blanche had gone and Clyde followed her lead. Sure enough, the outlaws came upon Blanche, running hysterically down the road. She continued to scream frantically as the car drew near. In her fist, she clutched some of the cards she'd been playing with when the raid began. Clyde slowed down and Blanche was hauled on board.

With Blanche in the car, Clyde drove away from Joplin at top speed. He journeyed for hundreds of miles, back to Texas. The gang stopped at Amarillo to lick their wounds. Finally, W. D.'s injury was attended to.

"I got no medical attention of any kind…until Clyde bought some alcohol and Mercurochrome at Amarillo, Texas, and dressed my wound," W. D. said in his police confession. "We didn't go back to Joplin any more after this gun battle. But rambled around for several months through a good many states, Texas, Oklahoma, Kansas, Indiana and Louisiana."[3]

The failed ambush at Joplin left two dead lawmen. Constable Harryman was killed almost instantly while Detective McGinnis managed to linger for a few hours, only to die in the hospital. McGinnis was engaged to be married (for the second time) while Constable Harryman was married and had five kids.

The Joplin massacre secured Bonnie and Clyde's notoriety, though not in the way they might have expected. When police inspected the bullet-scarred apartment where the gang had been hiding out, they found a treasure trove of personal effects. Among other items, they uncovered Buck Barrow's wedding certificate and a copy of Bonnie's poem about Suicide Sal. Most important for Bonnie and Clyde's image, the police uncovered two rolls of undeveloped film. When the pictures were developed, they became some of the most iconic crime photos of all time.

The shots depicted Bonnie and Clyde in a variety of menacing poses, brandishing weapons and scowling at the camera. In one famous shot, Bonnie is shown with a cigar in her mouth, a pistol on her hip, and a foot on a car bumper. Another image depicted Bonnie holding a huge shotgun, pretending to "hold up" Clyde, who is standing right in front of her, arms limp at his side. Bonnie is reaching into Clyde's jacket with a free hand to seize a revolver. Apparently, most of these shots were taken by W. D.

Ironically, Bonnie didn't smoke cigars. The stogie in her mouth had been a prop, borrowed from Buck. No matter—after the pictures were published, Bonnie would forever be associated with cigars. Newspapers inevitably described her as the "cigar-chomping" girlfriend or "moll" of Clyde. Bonnie came to detest these pictures, swearing vehemently that she didn't smoke cigars (something she felt was unladylike).

The Joplin ambush did something else as well; it intractably linked Buck to the Barrow gang. It's unclear if Buck really wanted to convert Clyde or if he had intended all along to team up with him in criminal activities. Not that it mattered; Buck was now wanted as an accessory to murder. After Joplin, Buck had no choice but to stick with Clyde. Were Buck to turn himself in, he would probably be executed.[4]

Blanche's dire predictions had come true. Her man was a criminal again, thanks to his brother. Blanche was forced to adjust quickly to life on the road. In spite of her nervous, reserved nature, she became an integral member of the Barrow gang. Because police hadn't identified her, the gang used Blanche to pick up food and drop off laundry. When shopping for food, Blanche avoided anything that required thawing or lengthy baking. Because they couldn't light campfires (for fear of being detected), the Barrow gang subsisted on cheese, tinned meat, crackers, and unheated pork and beans.

After Joplin, the outlaws were extra-careful about where they camped. They largely avoided tourist camps, hotels, and motels. Typically, they spent their nights in lonely farmer's fields or forest clearings and slept in their vehicles. Given that they couldn't bathe or shower, keeping clean was a constant battle. At best, gang members could wash themselves in a lake or river (which were generally quite cold). The men in the group had to shave in cold water, rather than risk being identified in a barbershop. Needless to say, the gang's bathroom functions were usually done outdoors as well.

For all the discomforts, Clyde still managed to enjoy himself on the road. In the spring of 1933, for example, Clyde had great fun with an undertaker and his fiancée. He kidnapped the pair at gunpoint in Ruston, Louisiana, after stealing the man's car. Instead of torturing or killing his prisoners, Clyde bought the pair hamburgers. After having a nice nosh, Clyde drove the reluctant passengers around, then dropped them at the side of the road, unharmed.

While Clyde was busy kidnapping undertakers, Blanche was trying to arrange a family reunion. Blanche traveled by herself to West Dallas to pass on news about Bonnie and Clyde to their families and set up a meeting with the outlaws themselves. It was "red beans for dinner" again at the Parker and Barrow households.

The family get-together took place in Commerce, a small town northwest of Dallas. The Barrow gang met their clans near a bridge spanning a ravine. The reunion mostly took place inside cars. Bonnie, Clyde, and Buck talked to family members while sitting in various vehicles brought along for the occasion.

Bonnie and Clyde's families were not having an easy time of it. Emma Parker and Cumie Barrow, in particular, seemed worn out and anxious. This might have had something to do with the intense police surveillance they were occasionally subjected to. The cops kept close watch on both households from time to time, in hope of catching Bonnie and Clyde at home. The cops weren't the only ones scrutinizing the Barrow and Parker clans. Henry Barrow was having trouble keeping his gas station business afloat. Many locals refused to patronize the place, either out of fear or contempt. The station received attention of the negative sort and was routinely vandalized. Henry didn't complain, however, and didn't try to bring his renegade son to heel. As Henry frequently told inquiring police, there wasn't much he could do to get gun-toting Clyde to heed the law.

The bandits had other issues to consider. As Nell Cowan later recalled, Clyde seemed upset for having gotten Buck back into the crime business. Buck himself was fatalistic. He told his family he would likely "get the chair" (i.e., be executed) if caught.

Bonnie had an equally philosophical attitude about her chosen fate. She fully expected to be punished at some point for the gang's misdeeds. Emma Parker tried to convince her headstrong daughter to surrender. Bonnie didn't want any part of such a plan. She told her mother it was likely that Clyde would eventually be shot or caught. If he had to die, Bonnie wanted to be there with him.

After the meeting, the Barrow gang went their separate ways. Buck and Blanche went off to visit her parents in Missouri. Clyde and Bonnie, plus W. D., continued their nomadic existence.

The evening of June 10, 1933, found the trio driving through the Texas panhandle, on the way to a Barrow gang reunion in Oklahoma. They were near a town named Wellington, Texas. Clyde was at the wheel, and the car was going at full speed. Clyde intended to cross a bridge that spanned the Salt Fork River. At the last minute, Clyde noticed the bridge was out. A sign stated it was closed for repairs. Clyde violently spun the steering wheel to avoid the bridge. The car shrieked across the road and lurched down a steep embankment.

Clyde was tossed clear of the wreck He hadn't been hurt. Clyde tottered back to the badly damaged car and grabbed W. D., who was still inside. He pulled W. D. out, then tried to free Bonnie. No luck. She was stuck fast inside the wreck. The car burst into flames. Bonnie began screaming as the flames lapped at her skin. Clyde worked desperately to free her. Bonnie shrieked and begged Clyde to shoot her to end her agony. Fortunately for Bonnie, a pair of farmers heard her cries.

These farmers—identified as Steve Pritchard and Lonzo Carter, by a subsequent *New York Times* article—rushed to the scene to help. They assisted Clyde in releasing Bonnie from the vehicle, then carried her to a nearby farmhouse. The men took her inside and gingerly placed her on a bed. Mrs. Pritchard gently dabbed Bonnie's terrible burns with baking soda as W. D. and Clyde looked on.

The farmers were suspicious of the intruders. They carried guns and Clyde wouldn't hear of taking Bonnie to a hospital. Carter slipped away to contact police. Clyde and W. D. didn't notice. They stood transfixed, watching the farmwife treat Bonnie's burns. Her injuries were extremely serious; the skin had peeled off her right leg, from hip to ankle. Bone was visible in a few places. Bonnie's recuperation in the farmhouse was brief. There was a knock, and then the front door of the house began to slowly open. A thoroughly rattled W. D. fired his shotgun at the door. He managed to blast the hand of Pritchard's daughter-in-law, who had arrived to help. The young woman collapsed on the floor, her shrieks competing with Bonnie's. Farmer Steve leapt to comfort his wounded relative, as the outlaws made a run for it. Bonnie staggered after W. D. and Clyde as best she could, into the darkened yard.

The trio just about collided with two lawmen—Sheriff Dick Corey and Wellington City Marshal Paul Hardy. The pair had driven to the Pritchard residence in response to a report about armed strangers who had been in a car accident.

Unable to believe his luck, Clyde ambushed the lawmen. He leapt out of the darkness at them, weapon drawn. The startled cops were taken prisoner and disarmed. Clyde secured the men with their own handcuffs, then demanded they give up their police car. The cops were in no position to argue and meekly walked the trio to their cruiser.

Marshal Hardy was placed in the back, with Bonnie. She sprawled on the back seat, howling in pain. Horrified by her injuries, Marshal Hardy tried to comfort the badly burned woman. He stroked her head and whispered encouraging words to her.

With one captive cop in the back, the second lawman was told to take a seat up front, with W. D. and Clyde. Once everyone was aboard, Clyde took off for the gang reunion in Erick, Oklahoma. Marshal Hardy's attentiveness touched Clyde's heart. When he pulled off the road before reaching Erick, Clyde didn't kill the two men. Instead, he ripped some barbed wire from a fence and used it to tie the two cops to a tree. Once his prisoners were secure, Clyde drove on to his rendezvous with Buck and Blanche.

Needless to say, Blanche was horrified at Bonnie's condition. She climbed into the car to console Bonnie as best she could. The sight of Bonnie's charred flesh reminded Blanche how dangerous the path chosen by her husband was. The Barrow gang carefully moved Bonnie to the back of Buck's car, and then the gang departed. They drove to a tourist camp in Fort Smith, Arkansas. The plan was that Bonnie could recover there. Bonnie had no say in the matter; she was out of her mind with pain.

Entering a tourist camp was a major risk. Bonnie and Clyde were now a national news story. Someone at the camp could have easily identified the bandits and turned them in. Clyde didn't seem concerned. He hovered over Bonnie, showing her more tenderness than he ever had before. He did his best to make her comfortable and take her mind off her injuries.

A few days after arriving at the tourist camp, Clyde took another big gamble. He realized that his partner and lover was close to death. Risking exposure, Clyde arranged for a doctor to visit Bonnie at the tourist camp in Fort Smith.

The doctor (who evidently kept his mouth shut about the identities of his patients) suggested Bonnie didn't have long to live. A sobered Clyde decided to collect Bonnie's sister, Billie, from Dallas. Billie's husband was in jail, freeing her up to play nursemaid for Bonnie. Clyde departed from Fort Smith on June 19, 1933, and headed to Dallas at top speed. He convinced Billie to help out, then drove her to Fort Smith.

At first, Bonnie was too out of it to recognize her sister. After a couple of days, Bonnie came to. Once she understood that Billie was there to help, she began to recover. Bonnie was a demanding patient, but neither Billie nor Clyde minded. Clyde spent much of his time by her bedside, assisting her any way he could. That included giving a helping hand with basic hygiene. In the early stages of her recovery, the gang had to help Bonnie on and off the toilet. She was unable to walk on her own.

Given that Clyde was preoccupied with Bonnie's woes, it fell to W. D. and Buck to replenish the gang's dwindling capital. The two decided a robbery was in order. On June 23, 1933, the pair hit a Piggly Wiggly store in Fayetteville, Arkansas. They didn't make a clean getaway. Their car was spotted fleeing the scene. Tipsters informed the police of the make of the vehicle and the direction it was headed.

In Alma, Arkansas, Town Marshal Henry Humphrey decided to intercept the fleeing bandits. Marshal Humphrey might have been motivated by the fact that he had recently been tied up and threatened by a pair of thugs who robbed an Alma bank. With this humiliation fresh in his mind, the lawman went about establishing a roadblock. Once the roadblock was in place, Marshal Humphrey and a deputy stood and waited.

Around 6:30 P.M., on a warm night, the two lawmen noticed a car approaching. Marshal Humphrey recognized the driver. It was a friend of his. Behind this car, however, was a second vehicle, driven by Buck and W. D. The marshal tried to wave his friend through the roadblock. As the friend slowed down, the second car smashed into its back bumper. The two lawmen approached this errant vehicle, not realizing who was in it.

Buck and W. D. leapt from their car, guns blazing. Marshal Humphrey jolted as their bullets hit him. His deputy raced off to a farmhouse, to call for help. W. D. and Buck climbed into Marshal Humphrey's car and drove away, leaving the dying lawman behind.

W. D. and Buck had sense enough to ditch the stolen cop car as soon as they had gotten a fair distance from the roadblock. They ended up hitchhiking back to the Fort Smith tourist camp. A kindly farmer stopped and gave them a ride. In this manner, the two newly minted cop-killers returned to the Barrow gang hideout.

Clyde decided the time had come to leave the tourist camp. Bonnie had recovered sufficiently to be moved without causing too much discomfort. The only problem was that the Barrow gang was down to one car. They would have to leave the tourist camp in stages. In late June, Clyde drove Bonnie, Blanche, and Billie out of the camp and onto a nearby hilltop. He left the women there, then went back to pick up Buck and W. D. The gang hid out on the hilltop for a few days, during which time Clyde and W. D. went off to steal a second vehicle.

Clyde made a particularly impressive haul during a dash to Oklahoma. Not only did he steal a doctor's car, complete with a black medical bag, he broke into a National Guard armory.

"Clyde brought back so many guns it looked like a gun factory," W. D. told police in his confession. "There were some 46 government automatics, .45 [caliber] pistols, several rifles and two or three cases of ammunition for the pistols and rifles."[5]

Among the choicer weapons stolen by Clyde were some BARs. W. D. would later claim that Clyde customized one of these guns to make it even more lethal. According to W. D., Clyde sliced a few inches off the barrel and somehow welded three ammunition clips together. This do-it-yourself project dramatically increased the potency of the weapon. Thanks to his improvisation, Clyde could shoot his "scattergun," as W. D. called it, 56 times without reloading. Gun experts suggest W. D. might have been engaging in some outlaw whimsy. They doubt three BAR magazines could be joined together in such a manner or that such a jerry-rigged weapon could even be fired.[6]

In addition to stealing guns and cars, Clyde also had some family business to attend to. On June 26, 1933, he dropped Billie off at the train station in a small town north of Dallas. Billie got on the train and returned home. Clyde drove his gang to a tourist camp in Great Bend, Kansas. Bonnie was recovering nicely but her healing process was far from complete. Clyde wanted to make things as comfortable for her as possible, as she mended from her horrible injury.

NOTES

1. Buck Barrow's wanted poster can be seen online at http://texashideout.tripod.com/bc.htm.

2. W. D. Jones, "Riding with Bonnie and Clyde," *Playboy*, November 1968.

3. W. D. Jones, confession to police, November 18, 1933, at the Dallas County Sheriff's Office in Dallas, Texas.

4. The wanted poster bearing the description of Buck Barrow (identified as, "Melvin Ivan") offers a $600 reward for Buck and his brother. The poster indicates both brothers are wanted for murder. Despite this, it's unclear whether Buck fired a weapon in the failed police ambush at Joplin.

5. Jones, police confession.

6. The Web site http://texashideout.tripod.com/bc.htm offers a photo illustration of what this triple-magazine "scattergun" might have looked like.

Lovers, outlaws, criminals—Clyde
Barrow and Bonnie Parker. From the
collections of the Texas/Dallas History
and Archives Division, Dallas Public
Library.

Bonnie Parker was the woman at
the center of the Barrow gang. From the
collections of the Texas/Dallas History
and Archives Division, Dallas Public
Library.

Bonnie and Clyde standing in front of a stolen car. The couple loved being celebrities and constantly took photographs of themselves. From the collections of the Texas/Dallas History and Archives Division, Dallas Public Library.

Photograph of the six-man posse that tracked down Bonnie and Clyde, bringing their career to a violent end. Left to right, front row: Bob Alcorn, Henderson Jordan, Frank Hamer. Left to right, standing: Ted Hinton, Prentiss Oakley, Manny Gault. From the collections of the Texas/Dallas History and Archives Division, Dallas Public Library.

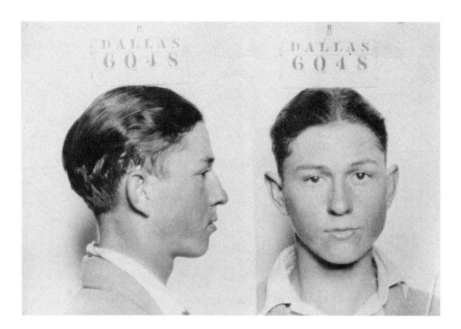

One of the first—but hardly the last—mug shots of Clyde Barrow. From the collections of the Texas/Dallas History and Archives Division, Dallas Public Library.

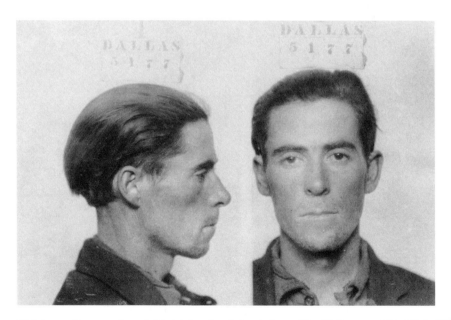

This is a police mug shot of Clyde's brother, Marvin Ivan "Buck" Barrow. From the collections of the Texas/Dallas History and Archives Division, Dallas Public Library.

Legendary lawman Frank Hamer is pictured here riding high in the saddle. Courtesy the Texas Ranger Hall of Fame and Museum, Waco, TX.

Police uncovered and displayed an arsenal of lethal weapons from inside the "death car." Courtesy the Texas Ranger Hall of Fame and Museum, Waco, TX.

Chapter 6

MAYHEM IN MISSOURI

Even as Bonnie recovered, the Barrow gang kept moving. In mid-July 1933, they left the tourist camp at Grand Bend, Kansas, and traveled to Platte City, Missouri. Along the way, they took the time to rob a few gas stations. Once they reached Platte City, the gang booked themselves into a small motel located behind the Red Crown Tavern. Bonnie, who was swathed in bandages, had to be helped from the car.

The Barrow gang rented two single-story cottages for the evening. Both cottages were made of brick and boasted a front door and a window. A two-car garage separated them. This garage could be accessed through a side door in each cottage. Besides offering comfortable accommodations, the motel had one other benefit; it was situated near the intersection for two highways—making getaways more convenient.

Once the gang was safely inside the cottages, Blanche was sent out to get some food. The Red Crown Tavern was a noted local eatery and teen dance spot, but Blanche didn't go there. Instead, she went to a nearby Slim's Castle (a combination gas station/restaurant) and picked up dinner and beer. The gang ate and then slept.

The next morning, Blanche was sent out again on another errand, this time to Platte City. W. D. was still hungry, however, so he went to Slim's Castle himself. It was not a wise move.

The gang was getting sloppy, exposing themselves to scrutiny. They should have been more careful—the presence of a tight-knit group of outsiders who were constantly coming and going raised eyebrows in the small town. Red Crown Tavern owner Emmett Breen became suspicious. He contacted Sheriff Coffey of Platte City, who duly showed up, along with a state highway patrolman. The two cops took a peak inside the garage that the Barrow gang was using. They took down the license plates of the vehicles parked there, and soon discovered that one of the cars had been stolen. The identity of the strangers in the two cottages remained a mystery, however.

Emmett begged the police to refrain from raiding the motel until diners and dancers at the tavern had left for the evening. The police politely gave in to this request, and waited until the Red Crown had emptied out. The lawmen didn't know whom they were dealing with, but they weren't taking any chances. The police called in an armored car to assist with their raid. Other officers were issued steel shields (to deflect bullets).

Around 11:00 P.M. on the night of July 19, 1933, the cops made their move. The armored car rolled up to the garage doors of the motel and stopped, a hulking metallic presence. Protecting himself with a shield, Sheriff Coffey cautiously stepped forward. He banged on the door of one of the cabins and loudly announced that the police had arrived. The sheriff demanded to be let in. "We had two cabins in the camp," W. D. told police in his confession. "Bonnie Parker and Clyde Barrow and I were in one cabin and Buck Barrow and Blanche had the other one. The officers went to Buck's cabin first."[1] Upon hearing the police at the door, Buck woke up in a start. Out in the yard, police heard Blanche trill, "Just a minute. Let me get dressed." Buck armed himself as a very nervous Blanche frantically packed.[2]

In the other cabin, Clyde was instantly alert. A light sleeper, Clyde had gone to bed fully dressed. He woke up the moment Sheriff Coffey began banging on Buck's door. Clyde hurriedly scooped up weapons and ammunition. He tore open the side door leading to the garage, and tossed a pile of guns into one of the gang's vehicles. The car was a Ford V-8. Clyde ordered W. D. to start it.

Outside, the police waited in the dark for something to happen. They didn't have to wait long. Clyde stood inside the garage, BAR in hand. He opened the garage door and peppered the assembled lawmen with .30–06 rounds. The police opened fire and the glass in the cabin windows exploded. Brick dust saturated the air as bullets smacked into the sides of the cottages. Standing almost within arm's reach of the garage, Sheriff Coffey took a bullet in the neck and collapsed.

Clyde reloaded and directed his fire toward the armored car. The BAR spat rifle bullets at the metal monster. Whether by accident or intent, Clyde aimed at the side door, one of the weak spots in the vehicle. The BAR rounds were so powerful they pierced the armored door and hit the driver in the leg. The driver screamed. Bullets ricocheted around the interior of the armored car as the driver let go of the wheel and cupped his wound.

Buck and Blanche rushed into the garage from their cottage. Buck had a pistol and fired at the cops. A shot from a policeman's gun hit him in the head and he stumbled, badly wounded. Blanche screamed and supported her husband. With W. D.'s assistance, she helped Buck into the car.

Bonnie clambered into the vehicle as best she could, hopping along on her badly injured leg as police bullets zipped around her. Clyde took the driver's seat, and W. D., armed with a Tommy gun, jumped on the running board. Clyde slammed down on the accelerator and the car shot forward like a rocket. W. D. held onto the vehicle with one hand and leveled his weapon with the other. He sprayed automatic fire at the dazed police to cover the gang's getaway. The armored car could have easily blocked Clyde's path. But the injured driver was in no shape to maneuver the metal behemoth. He groaned in his driver's seat and didn't try to ram Clyde's vehicle as it rocketed past.

Policemen on the ground turned their attention to the fleeing Ford V-8. Machine-gun fire from the cops blew out the back tires of the vehicle, but it kept racing forward. The bullets shattered the car windows, sending shards of glass flying everywhere. Some of them pierced Blanche's face, blinding her with blood. She howled in pain and fear. Her husband slumped next to her, half-conscious and bleeding heavily. Bonnie also sat in the back seat, face grim with pain and fear.

The bullet-ridden V-8 made it to a highway. Clyde drove down the road at full tilt, heart racing from their very narrow escape. "Clyde afterwards counted 14 or 15 bullet-holes in our car, but none of us was hit," W. D. later told police. "They did hit both the back tires, however, and they went flat after we had gone some distance."[3]

Back at the Red Crown Tavern, the police made no attempt to pursue the fleeing suspects. They were too busy trying to sort themselves out following the disastrous raid. None of the cops had been killed, which was the only bright spot in the evening.

After Clyde determined that the police weren't following them, he pulled the pockmarked V-8 over on a country road. He parked in a field and kept the car headlights on. With W. D.'s help, Clyde eased Buck and Blanche out of the car. He placed Buck on the ground in front of the vehicle, to inspect his wounds in the glare of the headlights. Buck was in very bad shape. His head wound was extremely serious; he was covered in blood and had gone unconscious. Clyde swabbed Buck's wounds with hydrogen peroxide and put bandages on his head. Buck groaned in his sleep.

Blanche was also severely injured. Flying glass had damaged her left eye. Beside herself with terror, Blanche screamed and wailed as Clyde tended to her wounds. He wiped the glass from her hair and face. Then, he drew some water from a nearby stream and gently dabbed her injuries. Clyde tried to calm his sister-in-law down. He gave her a pair of sunglasses to wear to protect her injured eye.

Having helped his comrades as best he could, Clyde walked to a nearby farmhouse. By the time he reached the house, it was midnight. Clyde hammered on the door until a sleepy farmer opened it. Clyde mumbled something about a car accident and asked for a jack so he could change a tire. The next morning, the farmer made an inspection of the area where the stranger said he was parked. The strangers were gone, but the farmer did find bloodstained bandages and newspapers. The farmer informed Platte City police of his discovery. The cops got a degree of satisfaction from knowing that the Barrow gang had not gotten away unscathed.

With three incapacitated people on his hands, Clyde continued to drive. He pulled over at one point to wash Blanche and Buck's wounds with water from a stream. He changed Buck's bandages and tried to make his brother comfortable.

Clyde was upset because he had left the stolen doctor's bag back at the motel. The bag contained painkillers and other necessary medical supplies. Buck was delirious and kept begging for water. Blanche pleaded with Clyde to take her husband to a hospital. Clyde made a difficult decision. Were Clyde to seek medical treatment for Buck, his brother would be recognized. Buck would end up in jail, where he'd probably be executed for participating in Barrow gang felonies. The way Clyde figured it, Buck had a slim chance of recovering on his own, without going to a hospital. It was a faint hope, but one that Clyde clung to.

Clyde drove into Iowa. Near a small village named Dexter, Clyde came upon a recreation area that consisted of expansive grasslands bordered by trees. Called Dexfield Park, this secluded locale was a popular spot for picnickers. Clyde decided it would do just fine as a temporary hideout. Clyde drove into the grasslands. He made some stops along the way, and eventually parked the vehicle in an isolated spot. Then, he and W. D. helped the three injured passengers out.

Once again, an attentive farmer betrayed the Barrow gang's whereabouts. The farmer in question was taking a stroll in Dexfield Park when he came upon bloodstained bandages and a floor mat belonging to a car. The items had been left behind by Clyde, en route to his final hiding spot. Normally, the farmer might not have thought anything of a few bandages and a car mat. However, just that day, he'd heard a radio report that the notorious Barrow gang might be in the area. His suspicions aroused, the farmer called the local Dexter sheriff to relay information about his find.

With the unsuccessful Red Crown Tavern raid in mind, the sheriff decided to proceed cautiously. He gathered his deputies together, then arranged a posse of local, rifle-toting citizens. The group slowly made their way into the forest that bordered Dexfield Park. The Barrow gang campsite was found relatively easily. To the sheriff's disappointment, Clyde was nowhere to be seen. He had left with W. D. to get food and steal new cars. The police and posse hid in the woods as they watched the campsite and waited for Clyde to return.

The lawmen observed Clyde and W. D. driving back to the camp in separate vehicles. The Dexter sheriff still hesitated to make a move. The police and vigilantes watched as Clyde lit a campfire when it became dark. Evidently, Clyde thought the gang was so well hidden that there was no need to keep a low profile. The fire provided warmth for the battered Barrow crew. Clyde passed food and drinks around and tried to boost morale. In the woods, many pairs of eyes watched everything he did.

During the night, Des Moines police, National Guardsmen, and local farmers armed with shotguns, complemented the posse and sheriff's men. A huge force slowly assembled in the woods, just out of view of the Barrow gang. Clyde remained oblivious to the small army of men gathering to kill or capture his gang. Throwing caution completely to the wind, Clyde and company hunkered down for the evening without posting a guard—their usual precaution when camping out. The enormous force, now more than 100 strong, waited and watched.

On the early morning of July 23, 1933, Clyde Barrow woke up and stretched. He informed Bonnie that he was going to bring Buck back home to their mother. It was a sign Clyde had given up trying to keep Buck alive. He was too far gone to help. Even with medical help, Buck probably wouldn't have survived much longer.

The campfire was relit and W. D. began roasting sausages. Bonnie began preparing coffee as Blanche fried eggs. Buck lay on the ground, groggy and drifting in and out of consciousness. In the midst of breakfast preparations, Bonnie looked up and realized the forest was full of men with guns. She cried a warning. Clyde and W. D. instantly dropped what they were doing and seized a pair of BARs. They raked the woods with automatic rifle fire, sending tree splinters flying. Bonnie fired as well as did Buck, despite his terrible injuries. Only half aware of what he was doing, Buck waved a pistol in the general direction of the woods and squeezed the trigger. Even Blanche allegedly shot at the attackers.

A barrage of bullets burst from the forest as the huge force returned fire. Some of the armed men steadied their weapons and poured lead at the Barrow gang campsite. Others charged forward, guns at the ready.

After shooting off a magazine, Clyde leapt into one of the cars on site and started the engine. As he did so, a bullet hit his arm. Clyde gasped and ran smack into a tree. The car was totaled. With rounds punching into the metal frame of the wrecked vehicle, Clyde jumped out. He raced toward the second vehicle, with W. D. right behind. Bonnie staggered after the men as best she could. Buck stood up and promptly took a bullet in the back. He fell to the ground, then weakly got up again. W. D. took a shot to the head but kept moving. The Barrow gang made it to the second car, but the posse's bullets riddled the windows and tires.

The crew exited the second vehicle. Buck collapsed again. He told Blanche to make a run for it, to leave him and get away. Blanche refused. Wearing the sunglasses Clyde had given her, she stood by her man, wailing as he staggered and bled. Amazingly, Buck continued to shoot at the posse with a revolver. The posse fired back. As Buck was shot again and again, Clyde, Bonnie, and W. D. raced into the woods.

Buck collapsed and his pistol went silent. Blanche knelt by her husband and cradled his bloodied body in her hands. She cried out at the attackers to stop firing. With her sunglasses still on her face, she looked like a blind woman comforting an injured lover. She told the police her man was dying and there was no need to keep shooting. Blanche wept as the enormous posse came closer. The armed men held their fire. A well-placed kick from a National Guardsman sent the revolver in Buck's hand flying. Other men picked Blanche up and pulled her from Buck. Blanche reportedly cried out to Buck, "Daddy, don't die—don't die."[4]

Clyde, Bonnie, and W. D. continued to sneak through the woods. They reached a river and waded in, only to be spotted by the posse. The latter started shooting at the three bandits. The gang kept going, however, and made it to the other side. Bonnie required assistance most of the way. W. D. carried her on his back as he waded across. Once they were out of the river, the trio continued their stumbling flight.

"We went about a quarter of a mile, up to a house, and Bonnie and I waited in the cornfield and Clyde went up to the house and put his gun on three men there and took their car and made them help put Bonnie Parker in the car and he and I got in and he drove off," W. D. told police.[5] The gun was waterlogged and out of bullets, but the farmers Clyde accosted didn't know that.

"We rode some distance and wound around through side roads and country roads for a distance of about 20 or 25 miles, and then we had a flat," W. D. continued, in his police confession. "In the gun battle back in the woods Clyde was hit several times, one through his right leg, one bullet grazed the side of his head. He had one buckshot in his right shoulder."[6]

Clyde was in considerable pain and let W. D. do some of the driving. W. D. was harboring some deep misgivings about the outlaw lifestyle. He kept his thoughts to himself, however, as the remaining members of the Barrow gang got as far away from Iowa as possible.

At some point, W. D. stopped the car so the gang could tidy up a bit. Bonnie cleaned the bloodied shirts of Clyde and W. D. The gang stole another vehicle, then drove it nonstop for three days. Clyde took over the driving, but had no real destination in mind.

After the Dexfield Park ambush, Blanche was put in a county jail in Adel, Iowa. She was later transferred to a prison in Des Moines. Doctors saw to Blanche's injuries, which were severe. She would never regain the use of her damaged left eye. Police also paid Blanche a great of attention. They avidly interviewed her about the Barrow gang's activities, with particular emphasis on the Joplin and Platte City ambushes. Even though she was half-blinded, a prisoner of the state and the wife of a dying man, Blanche didn't crack. The jumpiest member of the Barrow crew told police very little.

Buck, meanwhile, was moved from Dexfield Park to a hospital in Perry, Iowa. There, doctors did what they could to save him. Buck was kept in a locked, well-guarded hospital room. Police feared Clyde might try to spring his brother. While conscious, Buck talked a bit to police. He apparently admitted to murdering Marshal Henry Humphrey back in Alma.

On July 26, 1933, police permitted a visit from Buck's family. Cumie Barrow, Nell Cowan, plus a younger brother, along with Emma Parker and her daughter, Billie, gathered at Buck's bedside. While Buck managed to recognize his kin and even converse with them, it was obvious his condition was hopeless. Within hours of his family reunion, Buck's condition took a turn for the worse. Buck died at 2:00 P.M. on July 29, 1933. At 30 years old, Clyde's big brother was dead.

W. D. offered police and *Playboy* a detailed description of Bonnie and Clyde's post-Dexter movements.

"We traveled all around...through Nebraska, Minnesota and into Colorado," W. D. told police. "In Colorado, we saw a newspaper that said they were looking for us out there and we thought they were getting pretty hot on our trail, so Clyde turned back through Kansas and down into Missouri and back into Oklahoma and on across into Mississippi, about 40 miles from Clarksdale, Mississippi."[7]

Near Clarksdale, Clyde ordered W. D. to steal another car. This he did. Clyde then instructed W. D. to fill it up with gas. It was late July and W. D. was hot and weary.

"[Clyde] gave me $2.22 to get gas and sent me into a filling station and he was going to stop where he could watch me and told me to come back to him," W. D. related to police. "I bought five gallons, instead of filling it like he told me to, and I drove on up the road and he was supposed to follow me, but I turned off on a little country road. This was at night when I got on that country road, I cut my lights off and he didn't find me. I drove on a piece and got out and left the car and threw away a pistol and a big rifle I had with me and ran on across the country and put in most of the night running and early in the next morning, I got a ride on a truck into Clarksdale....I hoboed my way back to Dallas on freight trains. I stayed [there] a day or two and went down near Sugarland, Texas, to pick cotton."[8]

Stoop labor in the field seemed preferable to stealing cars and robbing grocery stores. "I'd had enough blood and hell," W. D. told *Playboy*.[9]

W. D. remained a free man for four months. In November, police received a tip that W. D. Jones had been spotted in Houston, Texas. He was working there for a vegetable peddler. W. D. was taken into police custody, where he proved extremely helpful. Only 17 years old at the time of his arrest, W. D. immediately abandoned any notion of "honor among thieves" and gave lawmen in the Dallas County Sheriff's Office a long, lurid confession. He claimed that Bonnie and Clyde had kept him as a prisoner and forced him to commit crimes. He admitted to taking part in gunfights but pleaded special consideration. W. D. claimed to have been asleep or injured and thus, "out of his head" whenever a shooting took place. W. D. also said he was delighted to be in custody, explaining that he was now safe from retribution at the hands of Clyde for abandoning the Barrow gang.

Life was equally tough for other Barrow gang associates. After being arrested in Michigan the previous year, Raymond Hamilton had been transferred to Texas. Throughout 1933, he was subjected to trial after trial for various Barrow gang offenses. It was as if the authorities, frustrated at their inability to hold Clyde accountable for his crimes, tried to be as tough as possible with one of his associates. By late August 1933, hapless Raymond had been sentenced to a total of 263 years in jail.

On August 8, 1933, Raymond was taken to the state penitentiary at Huntsville to serve out his term. He would eventually land at the Eastham prison farm, the same hellhole Clyde had been posted to. There, he was supposed to do his time, tilling the fields and picking cotton for two-and-a-half centuries or natural death.

Almost one month exactly after Raymond was shipped to Huntsville, Bonnie and Clyde paid a visit to their parents in Dallas. The latter were shocked at the extent of their injuries. Bonnie in particular was in rough shape. She was very thin, very scared, and needed help walking or going up stairs. Her burns had still not fully healed.

Clyde impressed the Parker clan by acting the complete gentleman around his partner. He served as her physical assistant, picking her up and carrying her around when she needed to be moved. Inside her mother's house, Bonnie lay on a quilt on the floor. She held hands with Emma Parker and spoke of her recent misadventures. Bonnie made it clear she and Clyde weren't sticking around for long. She asked if her mother had any extra pillows and blankets they could take with them on the road. Since Dexfield Park, Bonnie and Clyde had been living entirely out of a series of stolen cars. With fall approaching, Bonnie wanted to make herself more comfortable once they hit the road again.

In early September 1933, Blanche went on trial in Platte City. She didn't have an attorney to represent her. Blanche pled guilty to charges against her and received 10 years, to be served at a woman's prison in Jefferson City, Missouri. Throughout the trial, police maintained a large presence around the courthouse. They feared Clyde might try to bust his sister-in-law out of custody. Clyde never even tried. Even if he were physically able, Clyde wouldn't have bothered rescuing someone he never much cared for in the first place.

Bonnie and Clyde spent most of the fall recovering from their wounds. They lived in various Dallas-area hideouts and kept a very low profile. The pair kept in touch with their families and bided their time. After several weeks of rehabilitation, Bonnie and Clyde's funds were running low. As always when they found themselves in such a situation, their thoughts turned to robbery. They investigated possible targets, and eventually settled on an oil refinery near Overton, Texas. A little research indicated what day payroll was handled at the refinery.

In the brisk morning hours of November 8, 1933, Bonnie and Clyde plus a third man (whose identity remains a mystery to this day) drove up to the refinery in a Ford V-8. They entered owner Jim MacMurray's office with drawn guns. Clyde demanded the keys to the company safe. The latter consisted of a metal pipe with a hinged and locked lid. Said pipe was embedded in concrete in the floor, with only the lid showing. The refinery owner claimed he didn't have the key. In frustration, Clyde simply shot the lock off the metal pipe. He opened the lid and reached in, then pulled out a few thousand dollars. It was a big score by Bonnie and Clyde's standards. Bonnie, who had slipped outside, pulled up in the getaway car. Clyde and his unidentified partner in crime rushed out of the office and into the car. It was Bonnie and Clyde's first successful heist in months. The fact no one was shot or killed was also impressive.

Before Clyde could plan any more heists, he and Bonnie came very close to being captured. In late November, Sheriff Smoot Schmid of Dallas received a tip from a local farmer about unusual activity on a lonely country road near his property. The farmer had seen cars parked on this road several times and speculated (correctly as it turned out) that they belonged to the Barrow gang and their family members. Sheriff Schmid decided an ambush was in order.

During the evening of November 22, 1933, the sheriff and some companions set up a rough camp near the country road where the Barrow crew had been spotted. The men made sure their cars were parked far away from the camp, so they couldn't be seen. The sheriff's comrades-in-arms consisted of Deputy Ted Hinton, Bob Alcorn, and Ed Caster. Hinton was armed with a submachine gun, Alcorn had an automatic rifle, and Caster brandished a repeating rifle.

Sheriff Schmid's plan went as follows: The lawmen would wait behind a fence until Bonnie and Clyde pulled up close in their cars. Once a positive visual identification had been made, the police would leap out from their cover and demand that the bandits surrender. Hinton wasn't sure about the plan, noting that Clyde was awfully good at getting out of bad situations. Sheriff Schmid put such worries aside. He was sure Clyde would be sufficiently shocked and awed to surrender.

A few hours after the police set up their ambush, headlights could be seen from an approaching car. The vehicle contained Emma Parker and Cumie Barrow. The police watched the car go down a laneway located about 75 feet from the main highway. The roadway in question had a small bridge on it.

After a few minutes, another car came into sight. The vehicle drove past the parked car containing the outlaws' mothers. In the illumination provided by the parked car's headlights, the police recognized the faces of Bonnie and Clyde. Cumie and Emma snapped off their car lights as their offspring drove by.

It was at this point that the police made their presence known. They jumped from cover and fired a few warning shots. The lawmen aimed their weapons at Clyde's car and made menacing noises about what would happen if he didn't give up. At the sound of the gunshots, Clyde immediately went into action. He began driving evasively, and turned the car completely around. He tore off, down the roadway to the bridge.

The spinning car tires kicked up a cyclone of dust and dirt. Bonnie broke the glass in the back window with a gun, then aimed it at the cops.

Clyde could see the lawmen in the glare of his car lights. He took out a pistol and began shooting at the police with his left hand while steering with his right. Sheriff Schmid and his deputies blasted away at the swerving vehicle. One shot punctured a tire. Reduced to three wheels, the car kept tearing forward. Another shot hit Clyde in the legs. He grunted in pain, but didn't stop driving. He eased the damaged vehicle onto the highway. Once he was sufficiently far away from the rendezvous point, he ditched the car. Clyde stood on the highway and pulled out his gun. He forced a Ford coupe to pull over, then commandeered the vehicle. Sitting jauntily in the freshly hijacked Ford, Bonnie and Clyde raced off to Oklahoma.

The chagrined lawmen soon recovered the car Clyde had abandoned in favor of the Ford coupe. Inside the vehicle, the cops found food, magazines, and a variety of license plates and spent cartridge cases. But their main prize—Bonnie and Clyde themselves—had eluded them once more. Sheriff Schmid made a grim conclusion; the ambush had failed because the cops gave a warning. Next time, there would be no warning, only the sounds of guns talking.

Shortly after the unsuccessful ambush, Raymond Hamilton decided to bust out of the Eastham prison farm. He sought out a con who was up for parole and cut him a deal. The con's name was James Mullen. James was instructed to pass a message to Clyde. The message was that Raymond was eager to escape and required Clyde's help. James was also told to smuggle some pistols onto prison property. In exchange for these services, Raymond would give James $1,000—provided his jailbreak was successful.[10]

After being paroled, James located Raymond's brother, Floyd Hamilton, in Dallas. Floyd was one of several people who assisted Bonnie and Clyde on the sly, delivering them food to various Dallas-area hideouts. Floyd heard James out, and then arranged for him to meet with Clyde. James repeated Raymond's request for Clyde's benefits.

Most outlaws would have scoffed at what Raymond was proposing. As James explained, Raymond wanted Clyde to stage a raid on Eastham in order for him to escape. It was a crazy mission that was full of risk, but Clyde readily agreed to help out. He was keen on doing more holdups but felt he needed a partner to back him up. Evidently, Bonnie (still on the mend) didn't fit the bill. Clyde didn't care for Raymond's personality, but he did admire his bank-robbing abilities.

With James's assistance, Clyde drove out to the Eastham farm prison property in the middle of the night. The two men cased the farm, making mental notes on good hiding spots and escape routes. They moved silently, to avoid attracting the attention of the guards. As per Raymond's instructions, James hid a pair of .45 automatics in a pile of brush. After that, the pair snuck back to Clyde's car and drove away from the prison farm.

The next visitor's day, Floyd Hamilton let his brother know that everything was in place. The guns were planted and Bonnie and Clyde were ready to bust Raymond out. A date was set and a time agreed upon.

Clyde was delighted by the prospect of such a daring mission. Raiding Eastham represented more than just the chance to work with a former partner. It would also mean the fulfillment of a very old dream, of breaking into jail and "rescuing" as many prisoners as possible.

NOTES

1. W. D. Jones, confession to police, November 18, 1933, at the Dallas County Sheriff's Office in Dallas, Texas.

2. John Treherne, *The Strange History of Bonnie and Clyde* (Briarcliff Manor, N.Y.: Cooper Square Press, 1984), p. 150.

3. Jones, police confession.

4. Treherne, *Strange History*, p. 157.

5. Jones, police confession.

6. Ibid.

7. Ibid.

8. Ibid.

9. W. D. Jones, "Riding with Bonnie and Clyde," *Playboy,* November 1968.

10. There is disagreement on the correct spelling of James Mullen's name. Some accounts give it as Mullins or Mullin.

Chapter 7

JAIL BREAK-IN

Clyde crouched in a weedy ditch, peering intently into the morning fog. Clyde cradled a Tommy gun in his hands. Visibility was low and Clyde could just barely make out a strand of trees in front of him. The trees marked the edge of the Eastham prison farm. On a road behind him, Bonnie was waiting in a car. Clyde couldn't see her through the fog, but he knew she was there.

James Mullen stood next to Clyde in the ditch, automatic pistol in hand. It was nearly 7:00 A.M., on the morning of January 16, 1934. The two men had determined that Raymond Hamilton's work detail would be laboring near their hiding spot that morning. The work detail's shift was supposed to start right at 7:00.

Clyde listened closely to the sound of boots tramping along the ground. The 17-man prison detail was approaching. Escorted by guards, the convicts were marched to within a few yards of the ditch. Guards barked orders as they prepared the men for tree cutting. Clyde and James bent down lower in the ditch. They caught glimpses of the work crew through gaps in the fog.

The "longarm man" that morning was named Joseph Crowson. He marched about, rifle at the ready. Another guard named Olan Bozeman kept watch on the prisoners from horseback. As axes began slicing at trees, Raymond and an accomplice, named Joe Palmer (who was serving a 25-year term), rushed to the pile of brush where James had hidden a pair of pistols. They dug through branches, leaves, and dirt and found the two .45s that had been planted there. They snatched up these weapons and opened fire on the guards. Crowson was struck in the stomach and head.

He fell to the ground, dazed and bleeding. Bozeman was also hit. He took a bullet in the hip but wasn't badly wounded.

Alerted by the gunfire, Bonnie leaned on the horn of the getaway car. The horn cut through the fog like a train whistle. The work detail broke down in bedlam. Some prisoners were paralyzed with shock and confusion. Others took advantage of the moment and rushed off in all directions, seeking to escape. Raymond and Joe fired a few more rounds, then dashed through the fog toward the road. They followed the sound of the car horn to its source.

Clyde fired "a withering blast of machine gun fire," as a subsequent Associated Press story put it, to cover their retreat. He aimed upward, at the trees. After shooting a few pines, Clyde stepped out of the ditch and ran to the road. James followed close behind. They dashed over to the car where Bonnie sounded the horn, then waited. After a moment or two, Raymond and Joe came into sight through the fog. The two cons spotted the getaway car and raced toward it, pistols in hand.[1]

Clyde frowned as he realized Raymond and Joe weren't alone. Three other prisoners had escaped with them. They were Henry Methvin, a young, thickset con with bad acne; Hilton Bybee; and J. B. French. All three were violent criminals. Hilton was serving life, while J. B. was doing 12 years, and Henry, 10. Henry had been sentenced for attacking an oil-field worker with a knife and stealing the man's car.

Raymond and Joe crowded around Clyde and James. Henry, Hilton, and J. B. stood to the side, looking anxious. A brief shouting match ensued. Raymond had no intention of sharing the getaway car with three additional prisoners. Clyde made a quick command decision. He said Henry, Hilton, and J. B. were welcome to join the escape wagon, and then ordered everyone into the car. The men obeyed, possibly because Clyde had a Tommy gun in his hands. Bonnie moved over as Clyde claimed the driver's seat. The five prisoners plus James fit into the car as best they could. They sat on each other's laps and tried not to elbow anyone in the face. Once the car doors slammed shut, Clyde revved up and tore off down the foggy road.

Once again, luck was on Clyde's side. He managed to elude roadblocks and police cruisers. He drove for about 250 miles and then dropped off Hilton and J. B. Clyde continued along country back roads until he ended up near Fort Worth, Texas. While Clyde and company escaped, Crowson lay dying in a Huntsville hospital.

Prison Governor Lee Simmons's anguish was mixed with fury for the bandits who had shot the guard. By talking to his staff and other authorities, Governor Simmons learned that Bonnie and Clyde were responsible for the breakout. He promised Crowson that he would do everything in his power to track his assailants down. Shortly after this promise was made, Crowson died.

So far, no one had managed to bring Bonnie and Clyde to heel. The pair had repeatedly foiled attempts by state and local police to bring them down. The feds hadn't been any more successful. The FBI (still called the Division of Investigation at the time) opened up a file on Bonnie and Clyde but that was about it.

New tactics were called for.

Governor Simmons had a plan but needed permission to put it into effect. The prison governor wanted to hire a pro to track down Bonnie and Clyde. His official title would be Special Investigator for the Texas Prison System. The investigator's sole mission would be to destroy the Barrow gang. Whoever took the position would have the full support of the Texas government and could call on assistance as needed.

Simmons would have to run this plan by the governor before putting it into effect. The official Texas governor at the time was Miriam ("Ma") Ferguson, the same woman who had previously pardoned Clyde Barrow's brother. Technically, Ma Ferguson was the top politician in the state. In truth, she co-ruled with her husband, James A. Ferguson. James Ferguson had served as Texas governor from 1915–1917. During his second term in office, he was impeached by the state legislature for misapplying public funds and failing to properly enforce Texas banking laws. He was convicted and resigned on August 25, 1917.

James Ferguson did not go quietly into retirement; instead, he convinced his wife to run for governor. He would rule through her. Ma Ferguson ran in 1924 under the catchy slogan, "Two governors for the price of one." She won and became the first woman elected governor in America. Once in office, Ma Ferguson relied heavily on her husband for guidance and advice. She was defeated in 1926 and re-elected in 1932.[2]

Fiscally conservative, Ma Ferguson was more broad-minded when it came to social issues. She opposed Prohibition and the Ku Klux Klan and was also well known for doling out pardons—up to 100 a month by some counts. In addition to being generous with pardons, Ma and James Ferguson had a reputation for corruption.

Simmons wasn't sure how the Fergusons would react to his proposal. Even if they liked the idea of hiring a special investigator, they might not appreciate the man Simmons had in mind for the job. The prison governor wanted the position to go to Frank Hamer, a veteran lawman formerly of the Texas Rangers. Pushing 50 years old, Hamer was rock tough and extremely proficient at killing criminals. Problem was, he hated the Fergusons, whom he regarded as the epitome of corruption.

The outfit Hamer had spent much of his career with had a legendary reputation. Founded in 1835, before Texas was even a state, the Rangers initially served as a quasi-military force. Their mission became more focused on law enforcement over the years, with jurisdiction across the state. The Rangers had an enormous array of responsibilities. First and foremost, they were charged with bringing order to the Wild West, as it existed in Texas. In this capacity, the Rangers battled bank robbers, train robbers, cattle thieves, Native Americans, Mexican bandits, and other assorted desperados. Among other famous cases, the Rangers faced off against gunfighter John Wesley Hardin and bank robber Sam Bass.[3]

By the turn of the twentieth century, the Wild West had more or less been tamed, but the Rangers kept extremely busy. They had to contend with cross-border raiders during the Mexican Revolution; gamblers, murderers, and con men during the oil boom after the First World War; and bootleggers and rumrunners during Prohibition. Like the Royal Canadian Mounted Police (RCMP) of Canada, the Rangers became closely associated with the turf they protected. They were seen as embodying certain Texan values, such as toughness, prowess with firearms, harsh justice, and a sense of duty.

Hamer was perhaps the best-known and most respected lawman who ever served as a Ranger. He was born in March 1884 in Fairview, Texas, where his father worked as a blacksmith. The father moved his family to Oxford, Texas, in Llano County around 1894. Hamer grew up strong and self-reliant. As a young boy, he enjoyed hunting in the backwoods. He would often camp out for weeks at a time, living off the land and shooting game for his meals. In this manly manner, he became a crack-shot. Hamer also worked in the family forge as a blacksmith, an experience that left him with taut muscles and admirable stamina. As a young man, Hamer stood over six feet tall. He was lean, taciturn, and tough.

In 1905, Hamer helped capture a horse thief, an act of courage that greatly impressed the local sheriff, a man named D. S. Barker. Sheriff Barker recommended that Hamer join the Texas Rangers, which he did the following year. Hamer's first duties involved patrolling the U.S.–Mexican border. Two years after joining, Hamer quit the Rangers, to serve as city marshal of Navasota, Texas. Navasota was a very rough town that Hamer helped tame through a liberal application of two-fisted justice. Hamer worked as a "special officer" in Houston in 1911 and then rejoined the Rangers four years later. Hamer once more found himself patrolling the border, usually around the Brownsville area. In this role, he dealt with Mexican bandits and bootleggers.

New Year's Day 1922 saw Hamer transferred to Austin, Texas, where he served as a senior captain in the Rangers. Hamer's transfer coincided with a major oil boom in Texas. Oil towns became epicenters of crime. Newly wealthy Texans expended their money on various illegal diversions, including prostitution, gambling, and alcohol.

Hamer was ordered to calm down a town called Mexia. Prior to the discovery of oil, Mexia was a small community with a population of maybe 2,500 people. Once oil was discovered, Mexia's population exploded to 30,000 almost overnight, with a corresponding spike in vice. As a Ranger captain, Hamer made short work of the criminal elements in Mexia, often at the point of a gun.

Hamer's reputation for toughness, efficiency, and marksmanship continued to grow throughout the 1920s. He had few qualms about gunning down criminals in the line of duty. His weapon of choice was an engraved .45 caliber Colt single-action revolver that bore the nickname "Old Lucky." Hamer used this pistol and other armaments to kill dozens of bandits and bad men.

In 1925, Hamer quit the Rangers because he didn't care to serve under Ma Ferguson. Hamer made no attempt to hide his negative view of the new governor. The public wasn't ready to see Hamer go, however, and kicked up a fuss. As a result, Hamer came out of retirement and rejoined the force.

The year 1926 saw Hamer clamping down on crime in another Texas oil boomtown, called Borger. Once a quiet hick community, Borger's population soared to 45,000 with the advent of oil. Mixed in with oil workers and ordinary folks were a large number of hookers, roughnecks, card sharks, petty thieves, thugs, bootleggers, and drug dealers. According to Hamer's biography, Borger was known as "the most corrupt and violent town the state of Texas had ever seen."[4] Just as he had done in Mexia, Hamer's hardnosed tactics soon cleaned up Borger. Hamer's public stock continued to soar.

Hamer resigned from the Rangers once again in 1932, before Ma Ferguson returned to power. He took a job as special investigator for an oil company in Houston, but retained his Ranger commission. This meant he could still work as a government peace officer.

Hamer, by this point, had killed upward of 80 people. By floating his name past the Fergusons, Simmons was all but admitting he wanted Bonnie and Clyde exterminated. Somewhat to Simmons's surprise, the Fergusons were receptive to his pitch. The Fergusons didn't like Hamer, but they were canny politicians. They recognized the threat Bonnie and Clyde posed to people and property. The Barrow gang was bad for the state's image. Newspapers described Clyde as Texas' "number one desperado" and disparaged efforts by police to bring him to justice.[5]

The Fergusons approved Simmons's plan. Simmons was delighted. Now all he had to do was convince Hamer to take the job. Simmons visited Hamer at his home in Austin, Texas, on February 1, 1934. He had good reason to believe Hamer would turn him down. Not only did the lawman hate the Fergusons, but the bounty hunter position would entail a serious pay cut. Hamer was making $500 a month in his Houston security job. Simmons was offering him less than half that amount, for considerably more dangerous work.

The prison governor didn't try to sugarcoat the mission. When Hamer asked him how long it might take to track down Bonnie and Clyde, Simmons admitted that he didn't know. He suggested it might take as long as six months. It would take 30 days alone, estimated Simmons, for Hamer to acquaint himself with Bonnie and Clyde's movements and habits.

Hamer accepted the job. The low salary didn't deter him. Hamer hated criminals, loved a challenge, and had strong hunter-killer instincts. In this manner, Bonnie and Clyde acquired their most dogged and dangerous adversary.

While loath to talk to reporters, Hamer opened up to Texas Ranger historian Walter Prescott Webb, following the conclusion of his involvement with Bonnie and Clyde. He offered a wealth of detail about his mission.

"On February 10, 1934, I took the trail and followed it for exactly 102 days," Hamer told Webb. "Like Clyde Barrow, I used a Ford V-8 and like Clyde, I lived in the car most of the time."

Hamer told Webb that he studied Clyde's habits and interviewed people who knew him, in an attempt to get inside the outlaw's mind.

"I learned that Barrow never holed up in one place; he was always on the go; and he traveled farther in one day than any fugitive I have ever followed," said Hamer. "He thought nothing of driving 1,000 miles at a stretch. Barrow was also a master of side-roads, which made his movements irregular."

"I soon learned that Barrow played a circle from Dallas to Joplin, Missouri, to Louisiana and back to Dallas. Occasionally, he would vary the beat, but he always seemed to return, as most criminals do. [Bonnie and Clyde] would go to Indiana, Iowa or New Mexico, but like wild horses, they would circle to their old range," stated Hamer.[6]

Hamer did not work alone. After meeting with Smoot Schmid, it was decided that two of the sheriff's deputies—Ted Hinton and Bob Alcorn—would assist Hamer. Hamer soon learned that Hinton and Alcorn were good men to have around. They possessed firsthand knowledge of Bonnie and Clyde that would come in handy. Hamer also relied on help from his assistant, a lawman named Manny Gault.

The men met regularly, to discuss strategy and chase down leads. None of their comings and goings were public knowledge. Governor Simmons and Ma Ferguson wanted to keep Hamer's appointment a secret. No one wanted to tip off Bonnie and Clyde that Texas' most famous lawman was on their case.

As a result, the objects of Hamer's scrutiny remained oblivious to his attentions. If anything, Clyde felt on top of the world. The Eastham prison breakout had been a huge success. He had finally achieved his cherished goal of busting into jail and rescuing his peers.

Clyde was soon brought down to earth, however. Clyde might have been willing to risk life and limb to spring Raymond from jail, but that didn't mean he liked the man. Driving around with Clyde, Raymond kept up a constant stream of inane chatter. He offered wild ideas for future crimes and daydreamed out loud. Henry Methvin said little. He seemed thick-tongued in the presence of famous criminals such as Bonnie and Clyde. Joe Palmer remained equally quiet.

Clyde wanted to drive to Gibsland, Louisiana, to get in touch with Henry Methvin's father. Henry's father, Ivy Methvin, lived on an isolated farm. Always on the lookout for new hideouts, Clyde figured the Methvin spread might do just fine. Raymond had other ideas, however. As a recently sprung convict, Raymond was feeling randy. He wanted to meet a woman he knew named Mary O'Dare. Mary was married, but her husband was in jail. He'd been busted for various crimes and was serving a 50-year sentence.

Mary lived in Wichita Falls, Texas, near a newly established Barrow gang hideout in Vernon. Raymond, along with James Mullen, went off to visit Mary while the rest of the crew holed up at the hideout. Raymond's reunion with his ladylove went swimmingly. He managed to convince Mary to abandon her incarcerated husband and join the Barrow gang on the road.

Raymond traveled to Vernon and proudly presented his new girlfriend to his comrades. They were less than impressed. Mary had auburn hair and a very sexy nature. Clyde took something of an instant disliking to the woman. He didn't see the point in adding another moll to the gang. The presence of such a physically appealing young woman in such a tight-knit group caused tensions. Bonnie might have resented Mary's presence for a different reason. Unlike Blanche, Mary had a confident personality. She threatened Bonnie's position as top female in the gang.

The Barrow crew managed to put aside their differences to rob a National Guard armory on February 19, 1934. They absconded with automatic rifles, pistols, and plenty of ammunition. Shortly after the armory break-in, James bid adieu to his criminal comrades. He was confident that the now heavily armed Barrow gang could make good on the $1,000 owed to him for assisting in the Eastham breakout.

New weapons in hand, Clyde and his intrepid band of criminals held up a bank in the small town of Lancaster, located near Dallas. This was one of the gang's few bank jobs. Clyde used two vehicles for the rob-bery. One vehicle, containing himself and Raymond, was used for the actual robbery. A second vehicle, with Bonnie, Mary, and Joe was stashed in a secluded locale south of Dallas County. The heist went down without a hitch. There was no violent gunplay and Clyde and Raymond made off with several thousand dollars. The exact sum remains in dispute and was pegged somewhere between $2,400 and $6,700.

Clyde drove to the hiding spot where the second car was located. Bonnie had the car running by the time he arrived. Clyde took over the driver's seat and Raymond climbed aboard.

As they made their getaway, Clyde and Raymond got into a heated argument. Raymond thought the cash from the robbery should be divided 50/50 between himself and Clyde. The two men, after all, had done all the dangerous work. Clyde insisted on equal shares for everybody. Ray-mond grudgingly agreed to Clyde's division of the spoils. As the car raced along back roads, Clyde caught a glimpse in the rearview mirror of Ray-mond pocketing a few bills from the loot. More arguing ensued. Another version of the tale suggests that it was Raymond who was dividing up the money. In this take, Clyde became enraged when Raymond tried to give Mary a cut of the wealth. Regardless of who was counting the cash, it appears that Raymond alienated Clyde by filching some bills. Their criminal relationship was over, as far as Clyde was concerned.

In addition to pocketing more money than he deserved, Raymond had a tendency to whine and complain. He demanded that the Barrow gang do more lucrative robberies, instead of hitting up small-town gas stations and grocery stores. Raymond boasted of his ambition to be a major league bank robber. Clyde dismissed such lofty goals as unrealistic. He urged Raymond to focus on the job at hand and stop thinking of grandiose schemes.

On top of this, Mary was getting on everyone's nerves. She bickered a lot and had a disloyal personality. At one point, after Bonnie and Clyde got in an argument, Mary offered some unappreciated advice. Mary sidled up to Bonnie and suggested—only half-joking—that she poison her man or dope him up and steal his wallet. Bonnie was not amused.

In late February 1934, the Barrow gang drove to Oklahoma and then made their way to Missouri, Illinois, and Indiana. The crew hung out for a while in Terre Haute, Indiana, enjoying their newfound wealth, such as it was. They bought expensive clothes, and took chances being seen by going to restaurants and theatres. Meanwhile, tensions continued to simmer. Raymond didn't help matters by trying to flirt with Bonnie, as well as Mary. Needless to say, this didn't over well. Such behavior would have been unacceptable at a dinner party, much less among a crew of on-the-run criminals. Flirting with a woman whose man was handy with a Browning Automatic Rifle was downright suicidal.

To support himself in the manner he felt he deserved, Raymond committed a little larceny on the side. He robbed a bank in Grand Prairie, Texas, of $1,500 or so. "Raymond was after big dough," Hamer was quoted as saying in his biography. "He was not content to rob filling stations and live from day to day. He wanted a lot of money and to live in style. When Clyde refused to rob any more banks for a while, Raymond started in alone."[7]

By early March 1934, the Barrow gang was beginning to fall apart. Raymond and Mary took off in a huff back to Texas, in a car stolen especially for the occasion. The rest of the gang was alarmed. Clyde feared that Raymond might turn them in out of sheer spite. Clyde and company decided to return to Texas themselves. Bonnie and Clyde had a reunion with their parents and tried to forget about the recent unpleasantness with Raymond and Mary. Raymond, however, hated to be ignored.

Raymond wrote a letter to his Dallas lawyer, dissociating himself from Clyde. He portrayed himself as a put-upon "gentleman bandit," as Hamer put it, who wanted nothing to do with the Barrow gang. In his letter, Raymond denounced Clyde as a low-life thug who killed without hesitation or thought.[8]

Raymond's taunting letter ended up on the pages of several Dallas newspapers. Clyde read the letter and was infuriated. He secured a typewriter (most likely stolen) and bashed out a reply. The letter—with spelling mistakes corrected—reads as follows:

> So Raymond Hamilton never killed anybody. If he can make a jury believe that I'm willing to come in and be tried myself.... Ask him about that escape from Eastham farm where that guard was killed.... Well if he wasn't too dumb to know how to put a clip in an automatic... [he would have] fired a lot more shots and some of the rest of the guards would got killed too... it makes me sick to see a yellow punk like that playing baby

and making a jury cry over him. If he was half as smart as me
the officers couldn't catch him either. He stuck his fingerprints
on a letter so here's mine too, just to let you know this is on
the level. X Clyde.[9]

Clyde sent this missive to the Dallas assistant district attorney. He
enclosed a fingerprint on the letter so police could verify it was really
from him. This was not the only letter Clyde wrote that spring. He also
allegedly penned a note to Henry Ford, praising the automaker for his
cars. Clyde's letter read, "Dear Sir, While I still have got breath in my lungs
I will tell you what a dandy car you make. I have drove Fords exclusively
when I could get away with one. For sustained speed and freedom from
trouble the Ford has got every other car skinned and even if my business
hasn't been strictly legal it don't hurt anything to tell you what a fine car
you got in the V-8. Yours truly, Clyde Champion Barrow."[10]

While the letter to the Ford Motor Company has never been verified
and might just be a hoax (for one thing, Clyde's real middle name was said
to be "Chestnut," not "Champion"), Clyde's gripes to the assistant district
attorney had more far-reaching consequences.

By this point, Clyde was so fed up with Raymond he wanted to kill him.
According to one account, Clyde ordered Joe Palmer to track Raymond
down. When Clyde admitted he wanted to kill his former companion-
in-crime, Joe decided he'd had enough. He quit the gang—temporarily as
it turned out—reducing its core membership to Bonnie, Clyde, and Henry
Methvin. On the last day of March 1934, Clyde heard a report over his
car radio that Raymond and Mary had robbed a bank near Dallas. The
pair also allegedly kidnapped a young mother and her toddler son.

Clyde smiled to himself as he listened to the breathless news report.
He had a hunch as to where Raymond would head. He figured Raymond
would drive to a secluded spot north of Fort Worth and Dallas. The spot
was off the main highway, near the small community of Grapevine. It had
been used by Bonnie and Clyde for family reunions and would be an ideal
locale for a bank robber to hide out.

Clyde drove to Grapevine with Henry Methvin and an arsenal of lethal
weapons, including BARs. Bonnie was content to hold less dangerous
cargo. As Clyde plotted and drove, Bonnie stroked a white rabbit she
planned on giving to her mother. The outlaws had decided to make a day of
it; they would greet Raymond Hamilton, then visit their parents. Armed
to the teeth, Clyde drove to Grapevine to prepare a welcome for his former
comrade in crime.

NOTES

1. Associated Press, "Five Convicts Freed by Clyde Barrow," January 16, 1934.

2. For more information on the Fergusons and Texas governors, see the Texas State Library and Archives Commission Web site at www.tsl.state.tx.us/

3. Information about the Texas Rangers can be found at the Web site for the Texas Department of Public Safety at http://www.txdps.state.tx.us/director_staff/texas_rangers/

4. John H. Jenkins and H. Gordon Frost, *I'm Frank Hamer: The Life of a Texas Peace Officer* (Austin, Tex.: Pemberton Press, 1968), p. 143.

5. Associated Press, "Five Convicts."

6. Jenkins and Frost, *I'm Frank Hamer,* p. 210.

7. Ibid., p. 212.

8. Ibid.

9. Clyde Barrow's letter regarding Raymond Hamilton is reproduced in many sources, including John Treherne, *The Strange History of Bonnie and Clyde* (Briarcliff Manor, N.Y.: Cooper Square Press, 1984), p. 191, and Jenkins and Frost, *I'm Frank Hamer.*

10. For the letter Clyde allegedly wrote to the Ford Motor Company, see John Treherne, *The Strange History of Bonnie and Clyde* (Briarcliff Manor, N.Y.: Cooper Square Press, 1984), p. 95.

Chapter 8

SOUTHERN COMFORT

Three Texas constables zipped down Highway 114 near Grapevine, Texas, on bulky, police-issue motorcycles. The cops—Edward Bryan Wheeler, H. D. Murphy, and Polk Ivy—were members of the state highway patrol.

It was early morning and the patrolmen were on high alert. While it was Easter Sunday, the constables were preoccupied with secular thoughts. Raymond Hamilton—a known associate of the Barrow gang—had just robbed a bank. The motorcycle troopers were on the lookout for suspicious activity or vehicles.

The policemen rode past a black Ford V-8 parked on a side-road. A thickset young man was pacing outside the car. A petite young woman stood near him. To the police, it appeared that the car had broken down, leaving some stranded motorists by the road. They decided to take a closer look. Ivy continued along the highway while Wheeler and Murphy turned their bikes around to investigate. It was just a routine check, the sort of thing any conscientious cop would do. Ivy rode off as the other two troopers approached the parked Ford V-8.

The petite young woman watched fixedly as the two patrolmen came near. She began shouting, but the cops couldn't hear her above the roar of their bikes. The policemen left the main highway and parked their motorcycles. They began walking toward the car at a measured pace. Their pistols were still holstered. Neither man expected trouble.

At the sound of Bonnie's voice, Clyde sprang into action. He had been sleeping in the back of the car, exhausted after his fruitless vigil for Raymond Hamilton. Clyde snatched a sawed-off shotgun from the small arsenal of armaments inside the Ford. He slammed open the door, then dove out of the car, gun in hand. As Clyde positioned himself behind the vehicle, Henry Methvin seized an automatic rifle. Wheeler and Murphy reached for their pistols.

In spite of being rudely awoken, Clyde was in an expansive mood. It would be fun to take the two cops for a ride. The fugitives could start their day with a bit of kidnapping. Clyde stepped into view, shotgun in hand, followed at a stroke by Henry.

Clyde shouted, "Let's take 'em!" to his jittery comrade. Clyde would later claim that he meant, "Let's take 'em prisoner!" That wasn't what Henry heard, however. He thought Clyde was giving him an order to kill.[1]

Henry raised the BAR in his arms and fired a long burst. The .30–06 rounds from the Browning hit Constable Wheeler in the chest. The highway patrolman flew backward as the automatic rifle rounds tore into him. If Clyde was disappointed that his plan to kidnap the two cops had just been aborted, he didn't show it. A moment after Henry fired, Clyde raised his shotgun and blasted three slugs at Murphy. The trooper collapsed, next to his partner. The two policemen never had a chance—as the *New York Times* noted the day after the shooting, the patrolmen "died without drawing their revolvers."[2]

The Grapevine ambush came with its own grisly finale. According to legend, Bonnie personally administered a savage coup de grace to the fallen cops. A farmer named William Schieffer said he witnessed the whole thing. After the highway patrolmen were hit, Bonnie grabbed a pistol and purposely strolled over to the men. Bonnie allegedly shot each trooper in the head, gloating, "Look-a-there, his head bounced just like a rubber ball!"[3]

This account was based on the word of one witness, so it might be exaggerated or downright false. It certainly doesn't jibe with the testimony of captured Barrow gang members, who said they never saw Bonnie pull a trigger, much less commit double homicide.

Regardless of who fired what guns, the early-morning encounter between the Barrow gang and the law resulted in two more dead policemen. Once the shooting stopped, Clyde, Henry, and Bonnie climbed into the Ford V-8 and made tracks. In the driver's seat, as usual, Clyde raced the vehicle toward Oklahoma.

Ironically, Raymond Hamilton—the man Clyde intended to ambush by the side of the road—never bothered to make an appearance at Grapevine. In fact, there's no evidence to suggest that he ever intended go there.

The pointless ambush made Bonnie and Clyde more notorious than ever. The *Dallas Morning News* ran a bleak cartoon commemorating the attack. The cartoon featured a female figure bearing the words *the law* on her torso, staring forlornly at a fleeing vehicle. By the woman's feet were two dead policemen. The caption read, "Helpless?"[4]

A roadside memorial would later be erected in honor of the slain patrolmen. A plaque on the memorial reads as follows: "Troopers Wheeler and Murphy were shot to death Easter Sunday April 1, 1934, near this site on West Dove Road, by the notorious criminals, Bonnie Parker and Clyde Barrow. Wheeler and Murphy stopped their motorcycles near Parker and Barrow's car, thinking a motorist needed assistance. When they approached, they were shot...may God bless their souls."[5]

Less than a week after the Easter Sunday shootings, Bonnie and Clyde had another lethal confrontation with a pair of policemen. The second ambush took place April 6, 1934, in northeastern Oklahoma, where Clyde had been driving—rather aimlessly—since Grapevine. The countryside was flat and it had been raining. Clyde steered the car onto a side road and promptly got stuck in mud. Clyde and Henry got out of the stolen vehicle (a Ford V-8, of course) and pulled over a truck driver at gunpoint. They ordered the man to tow their vehicle out of the mud.

A passing motorist overheard Clyde and Henry barking threats at the truck driver. The same observant citizen noticed that the vehicle these men wanted towed from the mud sported a prominent bullet hole. The motorist reported his findings to the police, who decided to check in on things.

The two cops who investigated were Percy Boyd, police chief from Commerce, Oklahoma, and Constable Calvin Campbell. Boyd was in his 30s while Campbell, at 60 plus, was relatively ancient for a frontline policeman. Despite the age disparity, Boyd was Campbell's boss.

This mismatched pair drove to the location where the motorist said he witnessed the suspects threatening the truck driver. The police came upon a mud-splattered Ford V-8 and a couple of short-tempered men. A young woman was sitting in the front of the vehicle. The car had been successfully pulled from the muck and was ready to roll.

Boyd and Campbell parked their cruiser, then cautiously approached. Remembering the ambush at Grapevine less than a week prior, the two cops drew their weapons. Bonnie shouted a warning and Clyde and Henry reacted instantly. They grabbed the nearest weapons on hand—a pair of Browning Automatic Rifles—and let loose with a furious fusillade.

Campbell and Boyd snatched their .38 caliber police service revolvers out of their holsters and fired back. A .38 was no match for a BAR, however. Constable Campbell took a bullet in the chest that bored into his heart. He collapsed on the muddy road, dead already.

Police Chief Boyd was shot in the head. The bullet splashed blood all over the officer's face. Amazingly, it didn't kill him. Dazed, but alive,

Boyd let his pistol fall from his limp hand. He raised his arms in surrender. Delighted, Clyde leveled his rifle at the wounded chief. He commanded the man to come forward. Clyde smiled. Finally, a live policeman he could play with.

Clyde ordered the lawman to sit in the back seat of the Ford V-8. Boyd did as he was told. Henry sat down next to him. Boyd tried to blink away the blood that was falling in his eyes, and get a handle on the situation. Clyde carefully placed his rifle inside the Ford, then took the driver's seat. He drove away in a flurry of dirt, mud, and BAR casings.

At first, Chief Boyd wasn't sure who his assailants were. He was more concerned with his head wound in any case. Boyd placed a hand over the spot where the bullet had creased his skull in an attempt to stop the bleeding. Slowly, it dawned on Boyd that he was in the presence of Bonnie and Clyde. The Barrow gang, in fact, proved to be downright hospitable. Bonnie in particular was friendly and attentive. She chattered away at the astonished lawman as if he were a hitchhiker they had just picked up, not a badly injured cop whose partner was dead. Later, Boyd would say that Bonnie seemed happy to have someone new to talk to. Bonnie even apologized for killing Constable Campbell, as if his murder had been some minor social faux pas. Boyd gritted his teeth and accepted the apology.

The police chief did his best to make small talk with Bonnie and avoid making any sudden moves that might alarm the gang. At one point, Bonnie launched into a tirade about the media. She hated the way the press depicted her. The papers made her out to be some kind of sadistic she-devil, with a stogie constantly between her lips. An Associated Press wire service story about the Grapevine ambush, for example, described Bonnie as "the two-gun, cigar-smoking woman companion of Barrow." Such characterizations were flat-out wrong, Bonnie huffily informed the chief. For a start, she did not smoke cigars. Cigars were a man's treat. It was unladylike to smoke them. Boyd earnestly agreed that the press was disrespectful in its treatment of Bonnie. He promised to set the record straight, once he was free.[6]

Clyde entered Fort Scott, a small town in Kansas near the Missouri border. The gang bought a newspaper that contained a late-breaking story on Constable Campbell's murder and Chief Boyd's disappearance. For all of Bonnie's apparent hatred of the press, the Barrow gang loved to read about their exploits in the papers.

Bonnie and Clyde also purchased food while in Fort Scott. They retired to some nearby woods to eat. After having a good nosh, Clyde drove back to Fort Scott where he looked for a car to steal. To Clyde's disappointment, he couldn't find an appropriate vehicle. Bonnie continued babbling away with Chief Boyd. By this point, even Clyde was showing warm feelings for the wounded officer. Boyd had guts, thought Clyde. He admired the fact the chief hadn't panicked after being kidnapped.

Chief Boyd was eventually released unharmed. The chief contacted his headquarters to report he was still alive. Boyd was picked up by his fellow lawmen, and finally received medical treatment for his serious head injury. He told the cops what he knew about the Barrow gang. The chief also passed on the fact that Bonnie—contrary to her image in the media—didn't smoke cigars. Frank Hamer, Manny Gault, Ted Hinton, and Bob Alcorn met with Chief Boyd, to interview him about his ordeal.

Meanwhile, Clyde kept busy. On April 16, 1934, Clyde and Henry robbed a bank in Stuart, Iowa. The town was located close to Dexter, the community where Buck Barrow had been fatally wounded the year before. Clyde did not embrace the opportunity to revisit the site of his big brother's last stand. Instead, he drove to Joplin, Missouri, where he hooked up with Joe Palmer (who had evidently reconsidered his decision to leave the gang). Along with Joe and Henry, Bonnie and Clyde robbed a bank in Everly, Iowa, on May 3. The bank job went off smoothly, although the take—at around $700—was disappointing.

Following the Everly robbery, Clyde wanted to go to Louisiana to visit Henry's father, Ivy Methvin, at his small farm near Gibsland. Not everyone in the gang went along with this decision. Joe, for one, had no interest in going south. He was more intrigued by the World's Fair going on in Chicago. Clyde tried to convince him to stay but Joe was adamant. He left the gang for a second time, and Clyde, Bonnie, and Henry drove to Louisiana without him. The trio made it to Ivy Methvin's farm without incident. Ivy's farm was situated on sloped, wooded land. Where the trees had been cleared, Ivy grew cotton. The farm was isolated and could only be accessed via a single dirt road. Clyde figured the place would make a good hideout.

Methvin senior was none too thrilled by these developments. Ivy was extremely nervous to be around Clyde. He did his best to be polite but was highly relieved when Clyde took a sudden interest in an abandoned house located a few miles from the Methvin farm. The home in question was made of wood. It was old and unpainted and sat among a bunch of pine trees. A man named John Cole had owned the house. Four years prior to Clyde's arrival in Gibsland, Cole and his wife and two daughters died of tuberculosis in their home. As a result, none of the locals wanted anything to do with the place.

Like the Methvin farm, the John Cole house (as community residents referred it) could only be accessed by a single dirt road. Clyde liked the look and feel of the property. The fact its previous owner and his family died there, of TB no less, didn't bother him. Perhaps the Barrow gang could use the Cole house—rather than Ivy's farm—as their Louisiana hideout.

Homesteading wasn't the only thing on Clyde's mind: That spring, police arrested Mary O'Dare and Raymond Hamilton in Texas. O'Dare was picked up in Amarillo while Raymond was caught near Sherman on April 25, 1934. Raymond was in bad shape, having spent all his ill-gotten money. Raymond was wandering forlornly on foot when police nabbed him. Raymond offered no resistance. Police quoted him as saying, "I'm Raymond Hamilton and I don't intend to give you any trouble. I'm just fresh out of ammunition, money, whisky and women. Let's go to jail."[7] Clyde was delighted when he read about Raymond's capture. He gloated over his former partner-in-crime's sorry demise.

On May 6, 1934, Bonnie and Clyde held one of their secret family rendezvous, in a rural area near Dallas. The reunion was notable for its sense of foreboding. There was an unspoken realization that the Barrow gang couldn't continue for long. As their family members were well aware, Bonnie and Clyde had pushed their luck as far as it would go. For their part, Bonnie and Clyde were fatalistic, at ease with the prospect of death. "Mama, when they kill us, don't ever say anything ugly about Clyde," Bonnie allegedly told her mother.[8]

Bonnie's mother had other ideas. She begged Bonnie and Clyde to surrender, or flee to Mexico. A fast driver like Clyde could make the Texan-Mexican border in no time. Bonnie and Clyde weren't interested in fleeing, however, much less giving themselves up. It was as if they expected—maybe even welcomed—brutal punishment for their crimes.

Bonnie took the opportunity to present her mother with another self-penned poem. Her work was called "The Story of Bonnie and Clyde." It read:

"The Story of Bonnie and Clyde"

You've read the story of Jesse James—
Of how he lived and died;
If you're still in need
Of something to read,
Here's the story of Bonnie and Clyde.

Now Bonnie and Clyde are the Barrow gang,
I'm sure you all have read
How they rob and steal
And those who squeal
Are usually found dying or dead.

There's lots of untruths to these write-ups;
They're not so ruthless as that;
Their nature is raw;
They hate all the law—
The stool pigeons, spotters and rats.

They call them cold-blooded killers;
They say they are heartless and mean;
But I say this with pride
That I once knew Clyde
When he was honest and upright and clean.

But the laws fooled around
Kept taking him down
And locking him up in a cell.
Till he said to me,
"I'll never be free,
So I'll meet a few of them in hell."

The road was so dimly lighted;
There were no highway signs to guide;
But they made up their minds
If all roads were blind,
They wouldn't give up till they died.

The road gets dimmer and dimmer;
Sometimes you can hardly see;
But it's fight, man to man,
And do all you can,
For they know they can never be free.

From heartbreak some people have suffered;
From weariness some people have died;
But take it all in all,
Our troubles are small
Till we get like Bonnie and Clyde.

If a policeman is killed in Dallas,
And they have no clue or guide;
If they can't find a fiend
They just wipe their slate clean
And hang it on Bonnie and Clyde.

There's two crimes committed in America
Not accredited to the Barrow mob;
They had no hand
In the kidnap demand
Nor the Kansas City depot job.

A newsboy once said to his buddy;
"I wish old Clyde would get jumped;
In these awful hard times
We'd make a few dimes
If five or six cops would get bumped."

The police haven't got the report yet,
But Clyde called me up today;
He said, "Don't start any fights—
We aren't working nights—
We're joining the NRA."

From Irving to the West Dallas viaduct
Is known as the Great Divide
Where the women are kin
And the men are men
And they won't "stool" on Bonnie and Clyde.

If they try to act like citizens
And rent them a nice little flat,
About the third night
They're invited to fight
By a sub-gun's rat-tat-tat.

They don't think they're too tough or desperate,
They know that the law always wins;
They've been shot at before,
But they do not ignore
That death is the wages of sin.

Some day they'll go down together;
And they'll bury them side by side;
To few it'll be grief—
To the law a relief—
But it's death for Bonnie and Clyde.[9]

The poem was filled with allusions to political and criminal developments of the era. "The Kansas City depot job" was likely a reference to the notorious Kansas City Massacre of June 1933. The "kidnap demand" was a little harder to place, although it probably referred to the abduction of Charles Lindbergh III, the toddler son of famous aviator Charles Lindbergh. Charles was kidnapped in 1932, sparking a national media frenzy. When Bonnie wrote, "we're joining the NRA," she didn't mean the National Rifle Association, but rather, the National Recovery Administration—one of several New Deal agencies charged with alleviating the Great Depression.

There was one person in the Barrow gang who was not impressed by Bonnie's creative endeavors. This was Henry Methvin, who by then had become, more or less, a permanent member of Clyde's criminal crew. Henry was getting very antsy. He had teamed up with Clyde to acquire easy money and boss people around with guns. Dying in an apocalyptic battle with police was not part of the plan. In the days following the Bonnie and Clyde's family reunion, Henry began to ponder a future apart from the Barrow gang.

Clyde remained oblivious to his partner's discomfort. He drove around with no particular destination in mind for two weeks and kept out of public view. In late May 1934, Clyde decided to return to Louisiana, along with Bonnie and Henry. Clyde wanted to take up residence at the ramshackle Cole house. Everyone could take a well-deserved break while Clyde plotted the gang's next move.

Frank Hamer had a reputation for modesty. He never sold the movie rights to his life story, despite frequent offers. Nor did he ever write a book about pursuit of Bonnie and Clyde and other police matters. Hamer did open up to Texas Ranger historian Walter Prescott Webb, but his recollections must be taken with a grain of salt.

In interviews with Webb, Hamer gave the impression of being a super-sleuth. He claimed to have ferreted out Clyde's "mail box" or "post office" (i.e., a clandestine locale where he could give and receive messages from fellow gang members) in Louisiana.

"I learned that Clyde had his post office on a side road about eight miles from Plain Dealing, Louisiana," said Hamer. "It was under a board

[that] lay on the ground near a large stump of a pine tree. The point selected was on a knoll which Bonnie in the car could command a view of the road while Clyde went into the forest for his mail."

Hamer didn't explain how he uncovered this post office. For equally unclear reasons, Hamer said he deduced that Clyde would visit his post office around May 22. Accordingly, the posse drove out to Gibsland on the evening of May 22 and "made arrangement to furnish [Clyde] with more news than he ever received at one time," as Hamer put it.[10]

Other accounts omit any mention of a mailbox and focus on the Barrow gang's close family ties. Hamer is credited with correctly guessing that the Barrow crew would visit Ivy Methvin in Louisiana, following their family get-together in Dallas. In this telling of the tale, Hamer relayed his suspicions to Arcadia, Louisiana, Sheriff Henderson Jordan. Together with Hamer, Jordan and a handful of other lawmen laid a trap for Bonnie and Clyde near the John Cole house.

A new take on the demise of Bonnie and Clyde centers on an alleged confession from a turncoat. This version of events is based on formerly sealed FBI files, court documents, and comments from Hamer's own posse.[11]

In this take, the Methvins emerge as the main figures in Bonnie and Clyde's finale. According to this tale, Ivy Methvin asked a friend, John Joyner, to approach Sheriff Jordan with a proposal. Ivy wanted to meet the sheriff, with a view to bartering his son's freedom in exchange for important information on Bonnie and Clyde. Jordan and Ivy allegedly met in March 1934. Jordan knew Ivy's son was a criminal, but was surprised to discover he was part of the Barrow gang. The sheriff urged Ivy to convince his son to give himself up.

Ivy Methvin would have none of this. He pointed out that Clyde would not take kindly to a betrayal by one of his key gang members. Even if Henry was kept in protective custody, Ivy was sure Clyde would find a way to track him down and kill him. Given that Clyde had broken into Eastham prison to free Raymond Hamilton, it wasn't an unreasonable argument. Ivy wanted to cut a deal. If charges against Henry could be dropped—or at least, reduced—then the Methvins would help police locate Bonnie and Clyde.

Sheriff Jordan lacked the power to make such a deal. He said he would pass on Ivy's request to higher authorities. To this end, the sheriff contacted FBI offices in New Orleans. Jordan spoke to FBI Agent Lester Kendale. Kendale heard the sheriff out, then met him in person. The meeting was held in a rural locale in Bienville Parish. Frank Hamer and Bob Alcorn allegedly attended as well, along with John Joyner. Hamer apparently had no problem offering Henry a deal. In exchange for giving up Bonnie and Clyde, Henry would be granted partial clemency for his crimes.

Hamer relayed details about the deal to his superior, Prison Governor Lee Simmons. Simmons in turn ran the plan by Texas Governor Ma Ferguson. Ma Ferguson okayed the deal. Henry would be absolved of all criminal charges against him in Texas for his cooperation. He would still have to face charges stemming from the shooting of Constable Campbell in Oklahoma, but that was beyond the governor's scope. All of this allegedly took place prior to Bonnie and Clyde's Louisiana sojourn in late May 1934.

Throughout the spring of 1934, Sheriff Jordan kept in close contact with Ivy Methvin. He barraged him with questions about Bonnie and Clyde's habits and living arrangements in Louisiana. The sheriff tried to determine the best spot to confront the bandits. Thanks to Ivy, police now knew about the John Cole house. The lawmen wanted to wait until Clyde moved into the place, then raid it. Ivy thought this was a rash idea. Such a raid would only result in more dead policemen, he warned.

Hamer spent much of the spring hanging around Louisiana, waiting for the Barrow gang to make an appearance. In mid-May 1934, Hamer, Bob Alcorn, Manny Gault, and Ted Hinton took up residence in a Shreveport hotel. They played cards and wearily bided their time.

Clyde finally turned up in Louisiana on May 21, 1934. Henry wanted to see his father, so Clyde drove him to his dad's farm. Henry met his family in private. As Bonnie and Clyde waited in their car, Henry chatted nervously with his father (some accounts say he also conversed with his mother). It is unclear how much Henry knew about his father's negotiations with Sheriff Jordan. This would have been an appropriate time for Ivy to clue his son in. After Henry left, the Methvins contacted their intermediary, John Joyner. They told John to pass word to Sheriff Jordan that the Barrow gang was in town.

On May 22, Bonnie and Clyde drove into Shreveport to pick up some food. Clyde parked his car (a Ford, of course) by an eatery called the Majestic Café and sent Henry inside to place an order. While Henry spoke with the waitress across the lunch counter, Clyde noticed a police car. The vehicle was cruising by, uncomfortably close. Clyde panicked and raced away, abandoning Henry inside the café. Far from being upset, Henry realized he had been handed a golden opportunity. He wouldn't be anywhere near Bonnie and Clyde when the police ambushed the pair. Henry made sure that Clyde's vehicle was gone, and then cautiously exited the café. He walked out of Shreveport, then hitchhiked a ride to his brother's farm, located in Bienville Parish. With luck, Bonnie and Clyde would be out of his life forever.

As Henry contemplated his good fortune, the police prepared for action. On the evening of May 22, 1934, the lawmen gathered in Gibsland. Gault, Hinton, and Alcorn accompanied Hamer. Sheriff Jordan brought along his deputy, Prentiss Oakley.

The police decided to lay a trap for Bonnie and Clyde on the road near the John Cole house. In darkness, the law officers, plus Ivy Methvin (who was brought along to provide last-minute information), drove out to the abandoned property. They parked their cars so they were out of sight from the road, then went about choosing an appropriate locale for an ambush. They settled on a slight embankment covered in brush, which overlooked the road. This location offered good sight lines down both sides of the road. The lawmen could see for hundreds of yards in both directions. The Hamer-Jordan posse arranged themselves behind this brush.

The posse figured Clyde would arrive from the north, or to their right from where they faced the road. The lawmen were spaced out at 10-foot intervals along the embankment. Hamer was on the far left, followed by Gault, Jordan, Alcorn, Oakley, and Hinton.

Hamer, Gault, and Jordan were supposed to "take care" of whoever occupied the front seat of the car, while Oakley and Alcorn handled the back seat (if it was occupied). Hinton was to act as a "reserve"—applying gunfire or assistance where it was needed, said Hamer.[12]

The posse was armed with a variety of heavy-duty weapons. Hamer, for example, brought along a semiautomatic rifle customized to take a 20-round clip instead of its usual 5-round magazine. Hamer wanted to make sure he had plenty of bullets when he confronted Bonnie and Clyde. Hinton had a BAR and a movie camera with him. The other lawmen toted shotguns, rifles, and pistols.

Hamer would later claim he wanted to take Bonnie and Clyde alive. This seems unlikely; in fact, other accounts state Hamer was determined *not* to give a warning. As previous experience had indicated, Clyde was extremely quick on the draw. If ordered to surrender, Clyde might try to shoot it out instead. Understandably, this was a possibility the posse didn't want to face.

Once the lawmen were in place, they braced themselves for a long wait. The men endured mosquitoes, discomfort, lack of sleep, and boredom. Food consisted of grungy sandwiches from a bag. The lawmen tried to take shifts sleeping in their cars. A few vehicles went by, but they didn't contain the outlaws.

Ivy Methvin made the situation even more unbearable. He was having doubts about the whole affair and pleaded with the cops to call off the ambush. He was convinced everyone would be killed. To the posse's relief, Ivy left the ambush sight near the break of dawn on May 23, 1934. Irvin hadn't gone for good, however. He merely went to his farm to pick up an old beat-up truck. For some reason, Ivy drove this vehicle back to the ambush scene and continued to harangue the long-suffering lawmen.

Someone in the posse had an idea. Ivy was ordered to park his truck in such a way that it partly blocked the road. He was told to remove his left-front tire and jack the truck up. With luck, Clyde would recognize the truck, figure Ivy had tire trouble, and slow down to help out. At a dead crawl, Bonnie and Clyde could be picked off easily.

In his own late-life reminiscences, Hinton said that Ivy's reward for maneuvering the truck into place was to be handcuffed to a tree. As with many aspects of the demise of Bonnie and Clyde, several different reasons are offered as to why Irvin senior was cuffed. In one account, Ivy himself demanded to be handcuffed to a tree. That way, if the ambush failed he could claim to Clyde that the police had captured him and commandeered his truck. Another version states simply that the posse got so fed up with Ivy's whining, they cuffed him to a tree as punishment. It's also possible Ivy was manacled to keep him from breaking cover and giving away the lawmen's presence.[13]

By 9:00 A.M. on the morning of May 23, the posse was getting despondent. Despite their all-night stakeout, Clyde had yet to make an appearance. The police were sore, hungry, and covered in bug bites. Their nerves were frayed from being on constant alert for a car and the thought of coming face-to-face with a cop killer like Clyde. Their supply of food—such as it was—was running low, their patience almost exhausted. The lawmen decided to wait for 30 more minutes, then call it a day.

At 9:15 A.M., the policemen were startled to hear the sound of a car approaching at a rapid clip. When it was about 1,000 yards away, the car came into view. In later years, Hinton and Hamer would disagree on the color of the vehicle. Hinton said it was a tan-colored Ford V-8. Hamer said it was gray-colored. No matter.

The posse couldn't make out the occupants of the car, but they were sure it had to contain their prey. The lawmen tightened their grip on their weapons as Clyde breezed down the dirt road, toward a final reckoning.

NOTES

1. Clyde allegedly told his family about the roadside ambush and the miscommunication with Henry Methvin. Nell in turn told investigators. For more details, see John

Treherne, *The Strange History of Bonnie and Clyde* (Briarcliff Manor, N.Y.: Cooper Square Press, 1984), p. 181.

2. "Two Officers Slain; Barrow Sought," *New York Times*, April 2, 1934.

3. Treherne, *Strange History*, p. 17.

4. Editorial cartoon, *Dallas Morning News*, April 1934.

5. The roadside marker for troopers Edward Wheeler and H. D. Murphy can be seen at http://texashideout.tripod.com/bc.htm.

6. Associated Press, "Five Convicts Freed by Clyde Barrow," January 16, 1934.

7. Stone Wallace, *Dustbowl Desperadoes: Gangsters of the Dirty '30s* (Edmonton, Alb.: Folk Lore Publishing, 2003), p. 162.

8. Treherne, *Strange History*, p. 190.

9. Bonnie's poems are reproduced in multiple sources, including http://texashideout.tripod.com/bc.htm.

10. John H. Jenkins and H. Gordon Frost, *I'm Frank Hamer: The Life of a Texas Peace Officer* (Austin, Tex.: Pemberton Press, 1968), p. 222.

11. See Bryan Burrough, *Public Enemies: America's Greatest Crime Wave and the Birth of the FBI, 1933–1934* (New York: Penguin Books, 2004), p. 352–58, for a detailed account of the new version of Bonnie and Clyde's demise.

12. Jenkins and Frost, *I'm Frank Hamer*, p. 231.

13. L. J. "Boots" Hinton offers a very different take on the final chapter of the Barrow gang saga. Based on information from his father, Ted Hinton, Boots claims there was no deal with the Methvins. He says Ivy Methvin stumbled onto the ambush scene purely by accident; he didn't know the posse was there. Ivy was looking for his son, Henry. Henry apparently hadn't contacted him after breaking free of Bonnie and Clyde. The posse blocked the road with Ivy's truck, then handcuffed him to a tree to keep him out of sight as they waited for Bonnie and Clyde to arrive. Ted Hinton also claimed the posse set up their ambush on May 21, not May 22. This scenario is detailed in Ted Hinton's posthumous account of the Barrow gang's demise, *Ambush: The Real Story of Bonnie and Clyde* (Austin, Tex.: Shoal Creek, 1979).

Chapter 9

IT'S DEATH FOR BONNIE AND CLYDE

Clyde was driving, as always. Some reports state he was in bare feet. Others say he had simply taken off his shoes and was motoring along in stocking feet. A pair of sunglasses rested on the dashboard while various guns occupied the seats and floor. Bonnie was sitting contentedly in the back seat, munching on a sandwich purchased earlier that morning at Canfield's Café in Gibsland. Bonnie was wearing a red dress that matched her shoes. A road map of Louisiana was spread on her knees. She read a magazine as Clyde tore down the road. The two bandits were driving out to the John Cole house.

The car gradually slowed down as it approached Ivy Methvin's truck. Clyde moved into the left lane to avoid hitting the truck. By the time Clyde had reached the beat-up vehicle, he had decelerated to first gear. It's unclear if he recognized the truck as belonging to Henry's father. In the bushes, a mere 20 feet away, Sheriff Henderson Jordan watched, along with the rest of the posse.

Clyde looked to his left and to his right. No one was in sight. He couldn't see the owner of the truck anywhere. There was an embankment on the opposite side of the road from the stalled vehicle. It was directly to Clyde's left and covered in thick brush. As Bonnie chomped on her sandwich and read, Clyde scanned the brush for any signs of life. Seeing none, he prepared to drive around the truck in the road.

What happened next has been a source of conjecture for decades. Some accounts state that the posse simply opened fire all at once, blasting Bonnie and Clyde to pieces. L. J. Boots Hinton disputes this. He says Bob Alcorn called out from his hiding spot. The lawman ordered Clyde to "halt!"

A split-second later, deputy Prentiss Oakley thought he saw Clyde make a move. "Prentiss swore he saw a weapon coming [into view]," says Boots Hinton. "He popped off two rounds...and hit Clyde above the left eye."[1]

The rest of the posse joined in and the bushes erupted in gunfire. Bullets ripped into the car and its two passengers. The back of Clyde's head exploded in a plume of red. He slumped backward in his seat, as upholstery, blood, and lead flew around him. Bonnie was hit repeatedly and collapsed forward, her dress and flesh torn by high-caliber rounds. Bullets slammed through the car body as if it were made of tissue paper.[2]

Boots Hinton doesn't criticize his father and the rest of the posse for being so quick on the draw. "What ran through their minds, is the fact [Clyde] had gotten out of [several] scrapes," says Hinton. Thanks to quick shooting and driving, Clyde had continuously managed to elude capture in the past, even when it looked like police were on the verge of nailing him.

The police continued to pepper the Ford with round after round. Hinton unleashed an entire BAR magazine at the vehicle. Contrary to popular rumor, he did not film the actual ambush with the movie camera he had brought along. As Boots Hinton notes, "You can't hold a camera in one hand and a BAR in the other."

Clyde's foot slid off the clutch and the vehicle slowly careened forward. It ambled 30 yards down the road, rocketed by gunfire every foot of the way. The exterior of the Ford took on the appearance of a target in a shooting gallery. The car came to a stop in a ditch.

The police didn't stop shooting until they had expended their magazines. In total, they fired more than 150 rounds. The posse reloaded, then warily broke cover. Ears ringing from the brief cacophony, the lawmen approached the smoking Ford V-8. They kept their weapons trained on the crippled vehicle.

One of the posse members tried to open the bullet-marked door on the driver's side. It was wedged hard against the bank and wouldn't budge. The lawmen had to try another door to access the interior. Inside the car, the two outlaws were stone dead. Their blood was splattered everywhere. The Louisiana map Bonnie had been cradling in her lap had fallen to the floor. It was covered in gore. Bonnie herself was slumped forward, her tiny body bearing countless wounds. Her right hand had been shot off. Clyde was equally limp in the front seat. Both of the outlaws had been hit more than 50 times.

Satisfied their prey was dead, the posse inspected the Ford's contents. Along with the usual collection of food and garbage Bonnie and Clyde accumulated in all their vehicles, police discovered an astonishing array of firepower. The inventory of weapons included:

3 .30 caliber Browning Automatic Rifles
1 20 gauge sawed-off shotgun
1 10 gauge sawed-off shotgun
1 .32 caliber Colt automatic pistol
1 .380 caliber Colt automatic pistol
1 .45 caliber Colt automatic pistol
1 .45 caliber "double action" revolver
100 BAR clips of 20 bullets each
3,000 rounds of ammunition[3]

Police also found some nonlethal items in the car, including bags of clothes, a slew of license plates, and a saxophone that Clyde liked to toy with. It was the stockpiled weapons that primarily interested them, however. The ambush could have gone very differently had Clyde been given even a few seconds warning.

In interviews with Walter Prescott Webb, Hamer denied feeling any remorse for killing Bonnie, along with Clyde. He described his feelings upon looking inside the death car, at Bonnie's ragged frame. "I would have gotten sick, but when I thought about her crimes, I didn't," he told Webb. "I hated to shoot a woman—but I remembered the way in which Bonnie had taken part in the murder of nine peace officers. I remembered how she kicked the body of the highway patrolman at Grapevine and fired a bullet into his body as he lay on the ground."[4] This is, of course, assuming Bonnie really did administer the final fatal shots to the two downed patrolmen at Grapevine. Hamer seemed to have no doubts about the matter.

Hinton fetched his movie camera and shot footage of the wrecked car and the lifeless bodies inside it.

At some point, the posse remembered to free Ivy Methvin. Ivy had gone from wild anguish to burning anger. He was convinced the police had killed his son. He thought Henry was traveling with Bonnie and Clyde. Evidently, Henry hadn't contacted his family to let them know he had abandoned the Barrow gang for good. The police assured Ivy that his son had not been a passenger in the ill-fated Ford V-8. They showed Methvin senior the bodies of Bonnie and Clyde, which mollified him, temporarily. While pleased to discover his son was alive, Ivy soon began ranting anew. He cursed and screamed about his civil rights. He threatened to tell the FBI that he had been handcuffed to a tree against his will. Hamer took the man aside and did his best to calm him down.[5]

Bob Alcorn, Manny Gault, and Prentiss Oakley stood guard over Bonnie and Clyde's remains as the three other lawmen made the short journey into Arcadia. The posse needed to get the county coroner to examine the bodies. Someone also had to tow the death car from the ambush site.

Once he reached Arcadia, Hinton phoned Sheriff Smoot Schmid to inform him that Bonnie and Clyde had been killed. Hamer called Prison Governor Lee Simmons and passed on the same information. Upon hearing the news, Simmons immediately got into a car (driven by a prisoner chauffeur) and made tracks to the scene of the ambush. It was as if he had to see Bonnie and Clyde's bodies before he could accept that they were dead. They had managed to elude police so many times in the past, even in the face of overwhelming firepower, it seemed impossible they were gone.

Word of the ambush spread quickly among reporters. The Barrow gang's activities had been a huge news story in Texas and other Southwestern and Midwestern states. Even the venerable *New York Times* and other big-city Northern papers covered Bonnie and Clyde's crimes, along with those of their contemporaries.

One enterprising journalist contacted Emma Parker in West Dallas, to get a reaction statement from her. Mrs. Parker, however, was unaware her daughter was dead. She took the call at home, surrounded by her family. Pranksters phoned the families of Bonnie and Clyde all the time, claiming their kids were dead or in jail. Somehow, Emma knew this call was for real. She put the phone down, relayed the news to her family, then broke down and cried.

Back in Arcadia, a weird carnival atmosphere had descended. Reporters, locals, the curious, and the ghoulish all began to gather in town. Once the location of the ambush had been established, scores of people drove out to get a look. When Hamer, Hinton, and Jordan returned to the ambush site with the coroner, they were stunned to discover some 200 vehicles parked along the road. The three lawmen made their way back to their comrades with some difficulty. They weaved past countless cars and people on foot. A tow truck followed behind the vehicle containing the posse members.

The main body of the crowd was concentrated around Bonnie and Clyde's death car in the ditch. Alcorn, Gault, and Oakley did their best to maintain order, but it was impossible. They couldn't keep people away from the vehicle. Onlookers reached into the death car to feel Bonnie and Clyde's cold flesh. Some people snatched pieces of their clothes or hair for souvenirs. Other people picked up pieces of shattered glass from the windows and stole the vehicle's hubcaps. It began to rain, which added to the dismal ambience. At the center of the macabre exhibition, Alcorn, Gault, and Oakley stood fast.

Hamer's team connected with the three men guarding the car. Hamer, Hinton, and Jordan assisted in crowd-control duty as the coroner did a quick inspection of the bodies. He confirmed they were both very dead. The rain let up and a tow truck attached a cable to the battered Ford V-8.

A weird convoy took shape. Hamer, Gault, and the coroner headed up the front of the procession. Behind their vehicle came the tow truck hauling the death car (which still contained the corpses of Bonnie and Clyde). Behind the shattered remains of the death car followed a car containing the remaining lawmen.

And after them came a strange procession of civilians in their own vehicles, all vying for another glimpse of the car Bonnie and Clyde had died in and the policemen who had killed them. The convoy snaked its way around various back roads as it slowly crawled to Arcadia.

The convoy hit Arcadia around noon. It stopped outside the town funeral parlor (which also served as the local furniture store). The posse exited their vehicles and immediately stepped into another mob scene. People crushed all around the cars, shouting, snapping photos, and trying to get closer. Journalists scribbled in notepads while newspaper photographers captured the moment on film. The press of people was so intense, the posse had to force a path into the funeral home so the bodies of Bonnie and Clyde could be carried inside. The crowd cheered the lawmen. The lawmen, still exhausted, bug-bitten and tense, regarded the onlookers with disgust.

Once Bonnie and Clyde's remains had been moved into the funeral parlor, the milling mob surged round the bullet-ridden death car. For a second time, people began reaching inside the vehicle, to touch the mangled upholstery and seats. People took photographs of each other standing jauntily by the Ford V-8, creating grim keepsakes for their family photo albums. The car was eventually towed to a secure spot, behind a wire fence, near the town's jail.

That afternoon, Prison Governor Simmons showed up in his chauffeur-driven car. He had himself photographed with the victorious lawmen and offered them words of praise. Hamer cannily used the governor's presence to deflect any touchy questions about the ambush. By this point, some of the reporters were asking why the cops didn't issue more of a warning before opening fire. There was a sense that shooting a young woman—even one accused of being an accessory to murder, if not an outright killer herself—may have been a less-than-chivalrous act. "Now, here's the boss.

I've been acting on his instructions," Hamer told reporters. "If any statement is to be given out, he's the one to make it."[6]

Governor Simmons obligingly gave a little speech. For the first time, he acknowledged that Hamer had been specifically hired by the state of Texas to track down Bonnie and Clyde. As a glorified bounty hunter, Hamer was under no obligation to bring back his quarry alive.

There was one subject Simmons would not discuss. He demurred when asked by reporters what role the Methvins played in Bonnie and Clyde's violent end. According to journalists at the scene, Simmons sniffed, "There are some things which the public is not entitled to know."[7]

By dusk, sleepy Arcadia's population had swollen from 3,000 people to 12,000. All roads to the town were clogged with vehicles. Reporters continued to descend en masse. People pushed and shoved each other in order to get a chance to peak at Bonnie and Clyde's bodies. The latter had been placed in the backroom of the funeral parlor/furniture store.

Barrow and Parker family members began to show up. Henry Barrow arrived in the evening to collect his son's body. The normally unemotional man, who had moved his family from the bleak Texas countryside to the mean streets of Dallas in an attempt to improve their lot, was seen weeping. Buster Parker likewise drove in to take back the body of his sister, Bonnie.

The bodies were released to Henry and Buster the next morning. They were taken back individually to Dallas, where they ended up on display at separate funeral homes. Clyde was exhibited at the Sparkman-Holtz-Brand funeral parlor, while Bonnie ended up at the McKamy-Campbell Funeral Home. Embalmers carefully tidied up the corpses with makeup and other tools to disguise any bullet holes. Once again, the public streamed by to see the outlaw lovers in death.

There were few tears for Bonnie and Clyde in government circles. In fact, there was jubilation. Representative Robert Kleberg of Texas, for example, commended Hamer on the floor of the U.S. Congress. Far from criticizing the ex-Texas Ranger for shooting first, asking questions later, the congressman praised Hamer's two-fisted style.

"Mr. Speaker, my purpose in taking this fragment of time is to congratulate the nation, and the state of Texas and captain Frank Hamer, ex-Texas Ranger, and other officers who participated, for the work done in ridding their state of its public enemy number one, Clyde Barrow," stated Kleberg.[8]

In addition to Rep. Kleberg's fulsome praise, Congress passed a resolution, praising Hamer and the posse. For the moment, any qualms about Bonnie and Clyde's cold-blooded murder were put aside. Two dangerous criminals were dead. Their cop-killing rampage was over.

May 25, 1934, marked the day of Clyde's funeral. A big crowd gathered outside the chapel that had been selected for the dubious honor of seeing Clyde off. The mob was rowdy and noisy and issued taunts and insults to the Barrow clan. Clyde's body was taken from the chapel and buried in Western Heights Cemetery in Dallas. He wasn't buried next to Bonnie, but rather his dead older brother. Placing Clyde and Buck side by side was a bit of unintended irony. Clyde, after all, was directly responsible for Buck's death. If Buck had avoided his brother after getting out of prison, he might still be alive, living a virtuous life with Blanche. Henry and Cumie wept as Clyde was lowered into the ground.

One day later, Bonnie was buried. In death, she received a makeover. Her hair was done up, she got a manicure, and she was dressed in a blue silk outfit. Her body was placed in the oddly named Fishtrap Cemetery in West Dallas, next to some Parker relatives.

As the Parker and Barrow clans mourned, other citizens celebrated. The *Statesman*, a paper in Austin, Texas, declared May 28, 1934, to be "Hamer-Gault Hero Day." The day was supposed to feature testimonials about Hamer, a barbeque, and lots of speechifying by local dignitaries and politicians. Hamer, however, wasn't the slightest bit interested in being lionized. He might have felt guilty, recalling his handling of Ivy Methvin. Hamer-Gault Hero Day had to be cancelled when Hamer made it clear he wouldn't attend his own tribute. The *Statesman* sheepishly rescinded its plans for Hero Day.

Even in death, Bonnie and Clyde's relatives continued to pay for their association with the infamous pair. In February 1935, Cumie Barrow, Emma Parker, and more than a dozen other relatives and friends were put on trial in Dallas on federal charges of harboring Bonnie and Clyde. The charges stemmed from the fact that Bonnie and Clyde's families never turned them in. The clandestine reunions held over the years were seen as proof of the Barrow and Parker families' complicity. Male friends and family members of the Barrow gang were brought to court in chains, under the supervision of heavily armed federal officers.

When the trial began, the prosecution described Cumie as the "ringleader" of the effort to conceal Bonnie and Clyde from the law. Both Cumie and Emma gave similar testimony in their defense. They said strong family ties prevented them from giving police information on their kids' whereabouts. Cumie and Emma loved their children so much, they couldn't conceive of betraying them. The defense lawyer for Cumie took things a step further. In a florid address to the court, the attorney compared Cumie to the Virgin Mary watching her son die on the cross.

The jury didn't buy any of this. Both moms were found guilty. The presiding judge, one William Atwell, allowed the two women to pick their own sentence. Perhaps he was conflicted over the idea of parents being obliged to turn in their sons and daughters to police. Cumie and Emma ended up being sentenced to 30 days in jail.

Raymond Hamilton's mother also got 30 days. Billie Mace (Bonnie's sister), Mary O'Dare, and Blanche Barrow all got one year, plus a day. Blanche's sentence came on top of previous convictions for participating in Barrow gang shootouts. Clyde's sister, Marie Francis, got the oddball sentence of one hour, to be served in the custody of a U.S. marshal.

W. D. Jones also put in an appearance at the trial. He received two years plus a day for his part in harboring Bonnie and Clyde, to be added to time he was already serving for Barrow gang crimes. Interestingly, Nell Cowan was never put on trial for her part in protecting Bonnie and Clyde from the police.

Other family members and friends to receive federal sentences included Floyd Hamilton (two years); Clyde's younger brother, L. C. (one year plus a day), and his wife Audrey (15 days); Mary O'Dare's father, Joe Chambless (60 days); James Mullen (four months); and Steve Davis, stepfather of Raymond Hamilton (90 days). Hilton Bybee also got 90 days—a meaningless punishment given he already had a life sentence for an earlier conviction. These sentences were light, compared to what other former Barrow gang members received.

In late May 1934, Raymond Hamilton was shipped back to the Huntsville penitentiary. He was given an extra century, on top of his original 263-year term, for crimes committed after Clyde busted him loose. Joe Palmer was captured at some point during this period, in Missouri. Governor Simmons demanded that both men stand trial for killing prison guard Joseph Crowson during the breakout from Eastham farm. The men were tried and found guilty. They were both given a death sentence. It appeared that Simmons's promise to the dying Crowson would be fulfilled.

Joe and Raymond still had a few tricks up their sleeve, however. On July 22, 1934, the two men escaped from prison with the help of their fellow inmates and some .45 automatics, smuggled to them via a bribed guard. Other prisoners joined in as Joe and Raymond scrambled to freedom. In total, seven men tried to flee. A fire ladder was positioned against the outside prison wall. Raymond and Joe scrambled up the ladder and over the wall. When a third man tried to race up the ladder, an alert prison guard opened fire. Two of the escapees were hit. One died from his wounds.

Joe was quickly recaptured in August 1934, near Paducah, Kentucky. Police nabbed the fugitive while he was sleeping, a loaded .45 automatic within easy reach. Raymond fared longer on the outside. In February 1935, he robbed a National Guard armory in Beaumont, Texas, and made off with eight machine guns. Tommy gun in hand, Raymond robbed a bank in Mississippi on March 28, 1935. For this heist, he partnered with Clyde's old buddy, Ralph Fults.

Raymond's spree didn't last long. On April 6, 1935, Sheriff Schmid recaptured him. Raymond had disguised himself as a hobo and was walking with a gang of tramps when he was picked up. He offered no resistance. On May 10, 1935, Raymond and Joe were both executed in the electric chair, for the death of Joseph Crowson.

Of all the Barrow gang members and associates, Henry Methvin arguably had the most interesting time of it. According to a news story datelined from Austin, Texas, Governor Ma Ferguson granted Henry a "conditional pardon" on August 14, 1934. The pardon was given in exchange for "having furnished information which enabled officers to overtake Clyde Barrow and Bonnie Parker," stated the article. The news story made it clear that both Governor Simmons and Hamer were in favor of the pardon.[9]

Henry had been less than halfway into a 10-year sentence for theft and assault when he broke out of Eastham in January 1934, along with Raymond Hamilton. The pardon meant Henry wouldn't have to serve his remaining time. Presumably, the pardon also covered any supplemental sentence Henry would have received for his jailbreak.

A document detailing the conditional pardon makes no bones about Bonnie and Clyde's murder. In fact, it openly refers to the "justifiable killing" of the two outlaws. The document also states the pardon had been granted on the recommendation of Lee Simmons and Frank Hamer.

"It is provided that at all times in word and in deed [Henry Methvin] shall conduct himself as a good and law-abiding citizen and not again violate the laws of this state before the expiration of the term for which he was sentenced," states the pardon document. "If he is guilty of any misconduct or violation of the law, or for any other good and sufficient reason of the governor's justifying her in doing so, this pardon is subject to be revoked at the governor's discretion."[10]

As Henry was soon to discover, the conditional pardon did not amount to a "get-out-jail-free" card. Never terribly bright, Henry made an appearance at the office of Shreveport, Louisiana, Sheriff T. R. Hughes in early September 1934. "Thinking he was free of the law after a recent pardon by Gov. Miriam A. Ferguson of Texas, Methvin came to the sheriff's office here to obtain clothing which belonged to him, Barrow and Bonnie Parker," stated an Associated Press article on Henry's visit.[11]

Instead of receiving free clothing, Sheriff T. R. Hughes slapped Henry under arrest, for suspicion of robbing a bank in Montgomery, Louisiana. Police searched him and discovered a pistol on him. Henry found himself being questioned about the Grapevine, Texas, murders of highway patrolmen Murphy and Wheeler.

While Henry was never punished for his role in the Grapevine killing, he was held accountable for other crimes. Henry was a defendant at the "harboring" trial of Parker-Barrow relatives and gang associates. In spite of his later services in giving up Bonnie and Clyde, Henry received a federal sentence of two years plus a day (presumably for not ratting out Bonnie and Clyde until he'd been with them for months). Henry was then shipped to Oklahoma to face a state murder charge for the death of Constable Calvin Campbell.

Henry's trial took place in March 1935 in the district court of Ottawa County, Oklahoma. His defense was less than totally original. He claimed to have been sleeping in the car when Campbell was murdered. Henry fingered Clyde as the triggerman. It was a familiar excuse. When interrogated by police, W. D. Jones had said the exact same thing. Both men said they were slumbering when Clyde cut down policemen in their presence. Chief Boyd testified against Henry at the trial, but wasn't able to say for sure who killed his constable. The fatal shots might have come from either Henry or Clyde.

A mistrial ensued, when the jury couldn't decide on a verdict. A second trial was held in September 1935, at which Henry was found guilty and sentenced to death. The verdict was appealed, and in September 1936, the state criminal court of appeals tossed out Henry's death sentence. The court made this judgment based on the fact Henry assisted in bringing Bonnie and Clyde down. Henry's death sentence was commuted to life in prison.

This sentence didn't last either; in March 1942, Henry won parole. Described by Associated Press as "the dapper gunman who betrayed the notorious outlaw pair of Clyde Barrow and cigar-smoking Bonnie Parker," Henry walked out of jail in Oklahoma City.[12]

Six years later, Henry was back in the news. In April 1948, newspapers reported that Henry had been hit and killed by a train in Sulphur, Louisiana. The man whose inside information brought down America's most notorious criminal couple had allegedly been snoozing on the tracks when the train rolled over him. It was fitting end for someone who claimed to have slept through Clyde Barrow's last homicide.[13]

NOTES

1. L. J. "Boots" Hinton, interview with author, November 17, 2006.

2. Like everything about their last days, Bonnie and Clyde's grand finale is wrapped in speculation and confusion. Frank Hamer claimed that the lawmen gave a warning before firing, although his memory differed from that of Ted Hinton. Hamer said one of the posse members (he doesn't say who) shouted, "Stick 'em up!" Clyde allegedly ignored this command and made a grab for a gun, forcing the policemen to start shooting.

Another version posits Ivy Methvin as an active participant in the ambush. This take states Ivy was standing by his truck when Clyde pulled up. Clyde offered a greeting, Ivy ducked away, then Deputy Prentiss Oakley opened fire followed by the rest of the police.

In a third version, Bonnie spotted the posse in the bushes and yelled a warning. Before Clyde could react, the police started shooting.

3. Information on the death-car armory can be found in multiple sources, including Jay Robert Nash, *Look for the Woman: A Narrative Encyclopedia of Female Poisoners, Kidnappers, Thieves, Extortionists, Terrorists, Swindlers and Spies from Elizabethan Times to the Present* (London: Harrap, 1981) and http://texashideout.tripod.com/bc.htm.

4. John H. Jenkins and H. Gordon Frost, *I'm Frank Hamer: The Life of a Texas Peace Officer* (Austin, Tex.: Pemberton Press, 1968), p. 233.

5. Boots Hinton and a few other Barrow gang experts offer a very different take on the role of the Methvins in taking down Bonnie and Clyde. Boots says Frank Hamer offered an on-the-spot deal to Ivy Methvin: partial immunity for his son in exchange for not complaining about how the posse violated his civil rights. The "illegality of [Ivy's] capture" put Hamer in a tight spot, says Boots Hinton. In rushing to set up the ambush, Sheriff Henderson Jordan forgot to deputize the four lawmen from Texas. The latter therefore had no jurisdiction in Louisiana. The four Texans could have been charged with kidnapping Ivy Methvin. After gaining Ivy's silence, the posse members allegedly made a firm promise to each other. "The six officers had an agreement," says Boots Hinton. "As long as one of them was alive," they would remain silent about Irvin's kidnapping and the truth about the ambush. "The last man standing would set the record straight," adds Hinton.

6. Jenkins and Frost, *I'm Frank Hamer*, p. 236.

7. Ibid.

8. Ibid., p. 249.

9. Austin Bureau of the News, "Methvin Is Pardoned for Helping Officers Capture Clyde Barrow," August 14, 1934.

10. The document outlining Henry Methvin's conditional pardon can be viewed at the Web site, www.tmethvin.com/henry.

11. Associated Press, "Methvin Is Held for Questioning about Slaying," September 6, 1934.

12. Associated Press, "Man Who Put Clyde Barrow on Spot Freed," March 20, 1942.

13. Henry was "drunker than a jaywalking pissant," when he was killed, claims Boots Hinton. According to Hinton, Methvin became an alcoholic after leaving prison because the public falsely believed he had betrayed Bonnie and Clyde. Again, Boots Hinton insists that neither Henry nor Ivy Methvin cut any deal with the posse. The notion of a deal was to cover up for the fact Ivy had been handcuffed to a tree, says Boots.

Chapter 10

LIFE AFTER DEATH

The slide show was in full swing when Frank Hamer leapt to his feet. Accompanied by the faithful Manny Gault, Hamer charged to the front of the room. He snatched a handful of slides from the projector as the barker putting on the show gaped in shock. Slides in hand, Hamer smacked the barker and sent him flying.

It was early March 1935, and the crowd gathered in a room at an Austin car dealership had been watching a slide show featuring photos of Bonnie and Clyde's corpses. Hamer was incensed. He said he hadn't given permission for the Barrow gang ambush shots to be shown publicly. Of greater concern was the content of the promoter's presentation. The barker implied that Bonnie and Clyde's ambush was a cowardly act on the part of police. Even worse, the presenter claimed the Methvins had been paid to snitch.

"Neither I nor Mannie [sic] Gault ever saw Henry Methvin until three weeks ago," stated Hamer to reporters. The former Texas Ranger also took the time to issue a death threat against the man showing the slides. "I told [the promoter] if he ever showed those pictures again I would crawl on my knees to South America to kill him," Hamer huffed.[1]

While Hamer was successful in stopping the slide show, he couldn't stop every attempt to commemorate or cash in on the legacy of Bonnie and Clyde. Ted Hinton's 16 mm film of the ambush aftermath, for example, was quickly incorporated into a newsreel that had wide release. In pre-television days, newsreels offered moviegoers a quick summary of major events around the world. While the movie got wide exposure, L. J. Boots Hinton insists that his father "did not make any money from the film."[2]

A few months after Bonnie and Clyde's death, a book was published that put a positive spin on the outlaws' legacy. Entitled *Fugitives: The Story of Clyde Barrow and Bonnie Parker*, the book was allegedly written by Emma Parker and Nell Cowan. In reality, it was probably ghostwritten by a journalist named Jan Fortune. The book became notorious for its omissions and distorted take on history. It glossed over the fact that Clyde and Buck weren't the only jailbirds in the Barrow-Parker clans. *Fugitives* doesn't mention that Bonnie's first husband, Roy Thornton, was serving time when she met Clyde. Nor does it acknowledge that Clyde's brother, L. C. Barrow, was in jail in the period when the book was put together. The tome makes Clyde seem considerably more handsome and charming than he really was. It also pegs some of Clyde's killings (including the murders of John Bucher, Howard Hall, and Doyle Johnson) on other members of the gang, such as W. D. Jones.

It didn't take long for Hollywood to sense the commercial possibilities of the Bonnie and Clyde saga. *You Only Live Once*, directed by German émigré director Fritz Lang and starring Henry Fonda, was allegedly the first major film based on the Barrow gang. Released in 1937, the film centers on an outlaw couple called Eddie and Joan. The two go on a crime spree and become famous in the process. The couple is treated sympathetically, the implication being that societal pressures and a series of bad breaks forced them into a life of crime.

Meanwhile, Blanche Barrow, who really was forced into a life of crime against her will, quietly served out her sentence in the Missouri Penitentiary. She spent her time behind bars learning cosmetology and writing her memoirs. The latter would not see publication for decades to come. Blanche, who permanently lost sight in her left eye, was released from prison in March 1939.

"I want to forget all the past except the love I had for Buck when I met him in Dallas and we were married," Blanche told the *Dallas Morning News*. "I'm the only survivor of that quartet. I made my mistake and I paid the penalty. I don't intend to make the same error again. I'll keep away from West Dallas and make a new start." The article, which described Blanche as "still attractive despite the loss of an eye," focused on Blanche's claim of innocence. "I never had a gun in my hands," she was quoted as saying. "I never had done anything wrong but go along with [Buck] but I got my sentence."[3]

The man responsible for killing Blanche's brother-in-law died in 1955. It would be another decade before Frank Hamer's biography appeared in print, giving his take on the Barrow gang's demise.

The year 1958 saw the release of *The Bonnie Parker Story*. A classic B-film, the movie makes Bonnie out to be the cigar-chomping leader of the Barrow gang. Actress Dorothy Provine unsubtly played the Bonnie character. The movie changed the names of some of the major players in the Barrow saga. Clyde became "Guy Darrow" while his brother, Buck, became "Chuck." Names weren't the only thing falsified on screen; in addition to being a gun-wielding hellcat, Bonnie was depicted as a sex-starved vixen. Her partner in crime was inaccurately portrayed as a weedy wimp. A drive-in hit, the *Bonnie Parker Story* is dismissed by contemporary crime buffs as sheer fluff. "Story is wholly fictional and has more to do with showing Dorothy Provine in a tight sweater than with the real Bonnie," sniffs crime writer Rick Mattix, in an online review.[4]

In the early 1960s, interest in Bonnie and Clyde was renewed, following the publication of a book called *Dillinger Days* by John Toland. The book centered mainly on flamboyant bank robber John Dillinger, but contained enough Barrow gang material to intrigue the public. Two staffers at *Esquire* magazine—editor David Newman and art director Robert Benton—were particularly impressed. Benton had grown up in East Texas, and recalled his father telling tales about Bonnie and Clyde.

The *Esquire* staffers traveled to Texas and began interviewing people who knew Bonnie and Clyde. They did extensive additional research, then started hammering out a screenplay based on the outlaws' lives. Newman and Benton were heavily influenced by arty French films, and had no desire to make another B flick about the Barrows.

Their screenplay became the basis of *Bonnie and Clyde*, the classic 1967 movie. Featuring Faye Dunaway and Warren Beatty as the two outlaws, the film was brilliantly made and a huge hit. It launched the acting careers of Dunaway, Beatty, and supporting players such as Gene Hackman (who played Buck Barrow) and Michael J. Pollard (who played C. W. Moss, a composite of W. D. Jones and Henry Methvin). Estelle Parsons won an Academy Award for her screechy portrayal of Blanche Barrow.[5]

While wildly successful at the box office, the movie also proved highly controversial. The filmmakers were accused of glorifying a pair of low-rent, cop-killing holdup artists. Certainly there was no question Faye Dunaway and Warren Beatty were physically more attractive than their real-life counterparts. The film goes out of its way to glamorize its two leads (the movie opens with a nude shot of Dunaway lounging in her bedroom at her parent's house) while toning down Bonnie and Clyde's criminality. The Barrow gang is inaccurately depicted as primarily robbing banks. Most of the people they gun down are policemen, not unarmed store clerks and civilians. Frank Hamer is portrayed as a vengeful, repellent man complete with an old silent movie villain's moustache.

The film also became notorious for its level of on-screen violence (which was quite graphic for the times) and for typifying the popular 1960s attitude of living fast and dying young. It was such a pop culture sensation that *Time* magazine saw fit to put the movie on its December 8, 1967, cover for an article on new trends in American cinema.[6] *Bonnie and Clyde* popularized certain fashions (including Dunaway's beret and knee-length skirts) as well as bluegrass music (which was used throughout the movie for accompaniment).

While the film triggered a resurgence of interest in Bonnie and Clyde, it was widely panned by people whose lives were actually touched by the Barrow gang. Boots Hinton describes the movie as "five percent correct...[the filmmakers] exercised extreme artistic license." Both Boots and his father hated the movie: "If you wanted to see [Ted Hinton] explode, you just had to mention the film to him. It was like an atom bomb going off," recalls Boots Hinton. He says the film made him "furious." Among other sins, it portrayed Blanche Barrow "as a dimwit...Blanche was not a scatterbrain."[7]

While praising Estelle Parsons's acting skills, Debborah Moss, a first cousin of Blanche Barrow who resides in Fort Worth, Texas, also blasts the film. "[Blanche] was not the hysterical lunatic portrayed in the movie," says Moss.[8]

Prompted by the success of *Bonnie and Clyde*, a publisher called Pemberton Press released a biography of Frank Hamer in 1968. Entitled *I'm Frank Hamer*, the book includes several chapters devoted to the Barrow gang. This material was based on the interviews Hamer gave to Texas Ranger historian Walter Prescott Webb. Unsurprisingly, Hamer comes off looking good in this tome while Bonnie and Clyde fair badly. Some of the accuracy of the book has been contested, particularly with reference to the Methvins.

The same year as *I'm Frank Hamer* was released, *Playboy* magazine offered a rambling interview with W. D. Jones. W. D. offered up dollops of color commentary, much of which contradicted the statement he made to Dallas police after being captured. Life did not proceed smoothly for W. D. He was convicted in 1969 of possessing barbiturates and paid a $50 fine. This run-in with the law failed to make an impression on him. He was subsequently nailed with federal charges of illegally possessing 3,000 barbiturate capsules. In August 1974, W. D. was shot-gunned to death by an associate in Houston.

According to Boots Hinton, the six men involved in the ambush of Bonnie and Clyde had a long-standing agreement. They would wait until death had overcome all but one of their ranks before revealing the true story of the Barrow gang's demise. "The last man standing would set the record straight," explains Boots Hinton.

By the late 1970s, Ted Hinton had become the last man standing. He started putting together his memories of Bonnie and Clyde, with a view to publishing them. Hinton died of cancer in 1977, however, before his memoirs could be released. Following his death, Boots Hinton made sure his father's wishes were carried out. The end result was the publication of a book called *Ambush: The Real Story of Bonnie and Clyde*. Released in 1979 by a publisher called Shoal Creek, the book offered a controversial take on the end of the Barrow gang.

The book's main contention was that "there was no deal in place before the capture" of Ivy Methvin. The notion that the Methvins sold out the Barrow gang is false, Hinton states. While *Ambush* differs greatly from *I'm Frank Hamer*, Boots Hinton says his father was friends with the famous Texas Ranger. Ted Hinton even testified in court in support of a libel lawsuit launched by the Hamer family against the makers of *Bonnie and Clyde*. The suit was one of several initiated by surviving family members and Barrow gang associates.

Among other things, Ted Hinton testified that a scene in *Bonnie and Clyde* showing the outlaws capturing and tormenting Hamer was pure fiction. Ted Hinton apparently told the court that, "Nobody ever captured Frank Hamer except the Good Lord, and it's not clear He knew what to do with him." The Hamer family won their case and received a "six-figure" settlement, says Boots Hinton.

Ted Hinton's only child, Boots, was born in 1934. He followed in his father's footsteps, and served as a police officer in Irving, Texas. He later did work with the FBI and U.S. Customs Office. Among other chores, he did undercover narcotics operations in Mexico. While proud to have gotten his father's story published, Boots says he has no desire to write a book about his own life. "Half the stuff I've done, people wouldn't believe," he claims.

When he was 10 years old, Boots says his father took him aside to reveal the truth about Bonnie and Clyde's ambush. "Dad told me the whole story...then he told me what story I could say to reporters," he states. "I had to bite my tongue [for decades]." Boots says he currently has "three kids, two grandkids and two cats" and has outlived several wives. He describes himself as a "retired, old son-of-a-bitch."

That's not entirely true; Boots has a job, serving as the spokesman or "resident mouth" as he puts it, of the Bonnie and Clyde Ambush Museum. Opened in February 2005, the museum is located near Shreveport-Bossier City in Louisiana. "The museum occupies the exact historical location in Gibsland, Louisiana, of Ma Canfield's Café, where Bonnie and Clyde dined for the last time," reads online ad copy for the museum. "Here, you will experience a trip back to 1934 when the most notorious outlaw couple of all time met their bloody fate in a deadly ambush."

Boots Hinton says his father would have approved of the place. "Ted wanted a museum that told the actual story," says Boots, who refers to his father by his first name.[9] The Ambush Museum contains a wide variety of artifacts, including "seized weapons from Bonnie and Clyde's death car" and "exclusive film footage taken by the law enforcement posse immediately following the ambush," as stated in ad copy. Despite the Hintons' reservations about the film, one of the museum's main exhibits is the shot-up Ford V-8 featured in *Bonnie and Clyde*.

The Ambush Museum isn't the only institution dedicated to preserving the Barrow gang saga; there's also a museum in Dexter, Iowa, that details Bonnie and Clyde's ill-fated foray into that state.

The Barrow gang has a major presence in cyberspace as well. The Texas Hideout of Bonnie and Clyde (http://texashideout.tripod.com/bc.htm) was one of the first major Barrow-related sites to go online. Launched in 1997, site creator Frank Ballinger claims his pages get 6,000 hits a day. Ballinger lives in the western United States (he would rather not broadcast the exact locale) and heads a department for an engineering firm.

The Texas Hideout has an astonishing amount of Bonnie and Clyde information, from photographs, to documents and newspaper clippings. "In the beginning, I depended on books and 1930s newspaper articles for my information, but later got to know the family members of both the outlaws and also the lawmen who ended their lives," says Ballinger. "I've privately filed information that I don't post online out of respect for the families still living."

"What interests me most about Bonnie and Clyde is probably the love interest"—that is, Bonnie's incredible attachment to Clyde, says Ballinger. This love interest "was strong enough to make a well dressed woman with permed hair and high heels be willing to sleep in cars, in the woods, barns, etc., to be with her man," he states.[10]

Other Barrow gang associates also have Web sites devoted to them. For example, www.dazzled.com/blanche offers a detailed view of Blanche Barrow's life. It comes complete with family history and lots of flattering pictures. The site's logo consists of a pair of Browning Automatic Rifles positioned stock-to-stock and spouting flowers from their barrels.

The Blanche Barrow site went online January 20, 2006, roughly two decades after its subject passed away. The site was created by Moss, who works as a custom graphics designer and Web designer. Moss's motivation for going online is as unique as the spelling of her first name; she is determined to rehabilitate the image of her much-maligned relative. Moss believes Blanche was badly misrepresented by both the press and Hollywood.

"Blanche was a kind and loving wife and friend. Sadly, she fell in love with the wrong man and because of her loyalty to him, she was pulled into a life of crime when all she wanted was to live a normal life with her husband," says Moss. "She could have possibly left the group and turned herself in, but her love and loyalty toward Buck would not allow that to happen," Moss continues. "If anything happened to him, she wanted to be there with him. You know the rest."[11]

The site depicts a very attractive, bouncy Blanche. Many of the photographs were developed from Blanche's own personal negatives. The Blanche portrayed in the site is considerably different from the dumpy, middle-aged-looking matron in Bonnie and Clyde.

"Blanche Caldwell Barrow was raised in a loving, religious and law abiding home," reads a note on the site. "Then she met Marvin Ivan Barrow, brother of the notorious Clyde Barrow. They fell in love and got married. Because of her love and loyalty to her husband she spent four months of bloody hell on the run only to watch her husband dying of bullet wounds. She became a fugitive as a member of the 'Bloody Barrows,' otherwise known as the Bonnie and Clyde gang. She spent five and a half years in prison. A prisoner of love, all for the love of one man."[12]

Moss never actually met Blanche while she was still alive. She did, however, turn a bunch of tape-recorded reminiscences Blanche made in the 1980s into a CD. Moss edited the tapes and put them together in chronological order. The finished product is available on a disc called Blanche Barrow: A Voice from the Past.

In a similar manner, crime writer John Neal Phillips culled Blanche's prison memoirs into book form. Phillips edited Blanche's words and added information he dug up through his own research and interviews. The final product of Phillips's labors was a book, entitled My Life with Bonnie and Clyde. It was published in 2004, to generally favorable response.

For people who prefer their history raw and in the flesh, the community of Gibsland, Louisiana, holds an annual Bonnie and Clyde Festival. The event is held each year, "on the Saturday in May closest to the anniversary of [the outlaws'] shooting," according to a profile in American Bizarro (a compendium of off-beat people, events, and gatherings).

"A group of actors from Denton, Texas...show up annually to re-enact the scene with blazing guns and lots of fake blood," states American Bizarro. "Tourists can meet some of Bonnie and Clyde's relatives, such as Clyde nephew Buddy Barrow and his sister, Maude Barrow. Now and then some of Bonnie's kin show up as well. Then there's Boots Hinton, whose father Ted was one of the six lawmen who participated in the ambush." On top of this, amateur scholars and crime historians gather to debate various Bonnie and Clyde related issues.

Festival organizers are quick to point out that their two-day event is not intended to glorify Bonnie and Clyde. If anything, the festival is designed to celebrate the policemen who died in pursuit of Bonnie and Clyde and the lawmen who ended their crime spree. "We don't do it to honor Bonnie and Clyde," states festival organizer Billie Gene Poland in the *Bizarro* profile. "We do it as a re-enactment of history. And we let the law officers win at the end of the festival. It's not like we leave [the gangsters] going free or anything."[13]

Barrow gang Web site creators offer much the same explanation. "Anyone who reads my website will know that I do not glamorize Bonnie and Clyde," states Moss. "I just offer the facts, in the hopes that the younger generations will see the tragic outcome that a life of crime can produce. I neither praise nor condemn [Bonnie and Clyde's] actions. It is not my place to judge them without first walking in their shoes to see first hand why they did what they did."[14]

So why has the legend of Bonnie and Clyde endured, when the lives of so many other outlaws from the 1930s have been forgotten? "Tragic love stories have always endured—leaving their mark in history," notes Moss.[15] "Ted Hinton said that Bonnie and Clyde always put Romeo and Juliet to shame," adds Boots Hinton.[16]

Rick Mattix, a well-respected crime historian in Iowa, agrees. "I think the notion of a boy-girl bandit team struck some kind of romantic chord with a lot of people," says Mattix. He publishes a mail-order journal called *On the Spot*, which details crime and law-enforcement stories from 1920–1940. He recently co-authored a book called *The Complete Public Enemy Almanac*, which profiles a variety of bandits and criminals from the same period. He offers several additional reasons why the legacy of Bonnie and Clyde has endured. The number one reason is the fear (and awe) they inspired among the population at large.

"Unlike Dillinger, whose violent acts occurred mainly during bank robberies and encounters with police, the Barrows were likely to turn up anywhere at any time—at isolated farms, in small towns, etc.," says Mattix. "And of course, their main targets were stores and filling stations. So common people lived in dread of getting caught in the fire."

Bonnie and Clyde's violent deaths helped cement their myth. "They went out together in the proverbial hail of bullets...side by side to the bloody end. Almost a criminal version of Romeo and Juliet," states Mattix, in an echo of Boots's comments.[17]

Bonnie and Clyde's "ordinariness" also made them famous. "Bonnie and Clyde were not 'big' gangsters like Al Capone, but the 'people next door' type," says Ballinger. "The 'gun molls' of the bigger gangsters would never consider living like Bonnie did. They'd much prefer to stay at lavish hotels and dine in fancy restaurants."[18]

Ironically, Bonnie and Clyde's death car has found a home at just the sort of fancy resort the couple avoided in their lifetime. After being exhibited for decades at state fairs and other outdoor festivals, the battered Ford V-8 car was purchased by the Primm Valley Casino Resort. Situated approximately 35 miles south of Las Vegas on the Nevada/California border, Primm Valley offers gambling, an amusement park, fine dining, live music and comedy, golf, etc. The resort also features the Barrow gang death mobile behind glass. Primm Valley keeps the car on public display, along with Clyde's "death shirt" (the apparel he was wearing when shot dead).

The death car is beige in color and pockmarked with holes. There are virtually dozens of bullet-entry marks on the left side of the vehicle, evidence of the ferocious barrage that finally brought Bonnie and Clyde down. Tourists can see this car for themselves, in between rounds of gambling, golf, and dining—proof of the public's continued fascination with America's most notorious criminal couple.[19]

NOTES

1. Associated Press, "Hamer Breaks Barrow Slides at Lecture; Punches Operator," March 3, 1935.

2. L. J. "Boots" Hinton, telephone interview with author, November 17, 2006.

3. "Buck Barrow's Wife Finishes Prison Term," *Dallas Morning News*, March 26, 1939.

4. This review appears at www.dazzled.com/blanche.

5. For more information on the genesis of the *Bonnie and Clyde* screenplay, see Carol Polsgrove, *It Wasn't Pretty, Folks, but Didn't We Have Fun? Esquire in the Sixties* (New York: W. W. Norton & Company, 1995).

6. "The Shock of Freedom in Films," *Time*, December 8, 1967.

7. Hinton, interview with author, November 17, 2006.

8. Debborah Moss, e-mail interviews with author, November 15–16, 2006.

9. Hinton, interview with author, November 17, 2006.

10. Frank Ballinger, e-mail interviews with author, November 13–14, 2006.

11. Moss, interviews with author, November 15–16, 2006.

12. www.dazzled.com/blanche.

13. See Nelson Taylor, *American Bizarro: A Guide to Freaky Festivals, Groovy Gatherings, Kooky Contests and Other Strange Happenings across the U.S.A.* (New York: St. Martin's/ Griffin, 2000).

14. Moss, interviews with author, November 15–16, 2006.

15. Ibid.

16. Hinton, interview with author, November 17, 2006.

17. Rick Mattix, e-mail interviews with author, November 14–18 and 22, 2006.

18. Ballinger, interviews with author, November 13–14, 2006.

19. For a look at Bonnie and Clyde's death car, see www.primmvalleyresorts.com.

BIBLIOGRAPHY

PRINTED SOURCES

Agee, James, and Walker Evans. *Let Us Now Praise Famous Men*. Boston: Houghton Mifflin, 1939.

Barrow, Blanche Caldwell, and John Neal Phillips. *My Life with Bonnie and Clyde*. Norman: University of Oklahoma Press, 2004.

Brendon, Piers. *The Dark Valley: A Panorama of the 1930s*. London: Jonathan Cape, 2000.

Burrough, Bryan. *Public Enemies: America's Greatest Crime Wave and the Birth of the FBI, 1933–1934*. New York: Penguin Books, 2004.

Hinton, Ted, with Larry Grove. *Ambush: The Real Story of Bonnie and Clyde*. Austin, Tex.: Shoal Creek, 1979.

Jenkins, John H., and H. Gordon Frost. *I'm Frank Hamer: The Life of a Texas Peace Officer*. Austin, Tex.: Pemberton Press, 1968.

Knight, James R., with Jonathan Davis. *Bonnie and Clyde: A Twenty-First Century Update*. Austin, Tex.: Eakin Press, 2003.

Nash, Jay Robert. *Look for the Woman: A Narrative Encyclopedia of Female Poisoners, Kidnappers, Thieves, Extortionists, Terrorists, Swindlers and Spies from Elizabethan Times to the Present*. London: Harrap, 1981.

Newton, Michael. *The FBI Encyclopedia*. Jefferson, N.C.: McFarland & Company, 2003.

Polsgrove, Carol. *It Wasn't Pretty, Folks, but Didn't We Have Fun? Esquire in the Sixties*. New York: W. W. Norton & Company, 1995.

Steinbeck, John. *The Grapes of Wrath*. New York: Viking Press, 1939.

Stiles, T. J. *Jesse James: Last Rebel of the Civil War*. New York: Vintage Books, 2002.

Taylor, Nelson. *American Bizarro: A Guide to Freaky Festivals, Groovy Gatherings, Kooky Contests and Other Strange Happenings across the U.S.A.* New York: St. Martin's/Griffin, 2000.

Treherne, John. *The Strange History of Bonnie and Clyde.* Briarcliff Manor, N.Y.: Cooper Square Press, 1984.

Wallace, Stone. *Dustbowl Desperadoes: Gangsters of the Dirty '30s.* Edmonton, Alb.: Folk Lore Publishing, 2003.

ARTICLES

Associated Press. "Five Convicts Freed by Clyde Barrow." January 16, 1934.

———. "Hamer Breaks Barrow Slides at Lecture; Punches Operator." March 3, 1935.

———. "Man Who Put Clyde Barrow on Spot Freed." March 20, 1942.

———. "Methvin Is Held for Questioning about Slaying." September 6, 1934.

Austin Bureau of the News. "Methvin Is Pardoned for Helping Officers Capture Clyde Barrow." August 14, 1934.

"Buck Barrow's Wife Finishes Prison Term." *Dallas Morning News*, March 26, 1939.

Editorial cartoon. *Dallas Journal*, April 9, 1934.

Editorial cartoon. *Dallas Morning News*, April 1934.

"Father and Child Die of Pneumonia." *Dallas Times Herald*, January 28, 1923.

Jones, W. D. "Riding with Bonnie and Clyde." *Playboy*, November 1968. The interview is available online at http://www.cinetropic.com/janeloisemorris/commentary/bonn%26clyde/wdjones.html

Persell, Thomas. Interview by Perry Smith. *Springfield (MO) Press*, January 27, 1933.

"The Shock of Freedom in Films." *Time*, December 8, 1967.

True Detective Mysteries, November 1934. This issue contains a hard-to-find interview with Sheriff Jordan Henderson offering his take on the Bonnie and Clyde ambush.

"Two Officers Slain; Barrow Sought." *New York Times*, April 2, 1934.

WEB SITES

http://texashideout.tripod.com/bc.htm (highly recommended; excellent source of Bonnie and Clyde material)

www.onthespotjournal.com/journal.html (quarterly journal devoted to discussing crime-related personalities and issues from the 1920s and 1930s)

www.dazzled.com/blanche (a fascinating look at a little-known side of Blanche Barrow)

http://bonnieandclydemuseum.com (Bonnie and Clyde Ambush Museum; definitely worth a look for true crime aficionados) www.tsha.utexas.edu (a self-described "digital gateway to Texas history at the University of Texas at Austin")

www.tmethvin.com/henry (good source of newspaper articles regarding the Barrow gang)

www.dallashistory.org (Dallas Historical Society; offers basic background information on the Barrow gang saga)

www.dallaslibrary.org (Dallas Public Library; good source of Bonnie and Clyde photographs, including some of their most famous pictures)

www.auto-ordnance.com (excellent resource for information on Thompson submachine guns)

www.swhistorical.com (Southwestern Historical Society; for Bonnie and Clyde–related newsletters and tours)

www.texasranger.org/halloffame/Hamer_Frank.htm (information on Texas Rangers and Frank Hamer)

www.txdps.state.tx.us/director_staff/texas_rangers/ (Texas Department of Public Safety; contains additional information on the Texas Rangers)

www.tsl.state.tx.us/ (Texas State Library and Archives Commission; plentiful information on Texas governors)

www.crimelibrary.com (good—if not entirely accurate—summary of the Bonnie and Clyde story)

http://newdeal.feri.org/tva/tva10.htm (information on rural electrification and the New Deal)

www.fbi.gov (Federal Bureau of Investigation; contains information on the FBI's pursuit of Bonnie and Clyde, such as it was)

www.primmvalleyresorts.com (for a look at the Bonnie and Clyde death car)

INTERVIEWS WITH AUTHOR

Rick Mattix, e-mail interviews, November 14–18 and 22, 2006.

Jim Knight, e-mail interviews, November 24–26, 2006, and January 15, 2007.

Debborah Moss, e-mail interviews, November 15–16, 2006.

L. J. "Boots" Hinton, telephone interview, November 17, 2006.

Frank Ballinger, e-mail interviews, November 13–24, 2006.

ADDITIONAL SOURCES

The author made heavy use of the confession W. D. Jones offered to the Dallas County Sheriff's Office in Dallas, Texas, on November 18, 1933. This confession was available at http://texashideout.tripod.com/bc.htm but is no longer posted online.

The author made use of a research paper by Jim Knight entitled "Three Ambushes" that was presented at the Bonnie and Clyde Festival in Gibsland, Louisiana, May 19–20, 2006.

INDEX